Praise

*Good Things*

"Kevin Gerald isn't one of those annoying 'God is good . . . all the time . . . generically speaking' Christians. He champions an optimism that doesn't contradict reality. He acknowledges the frustrations of life but makes the convincing case that the force of God's favor is always greater. This is my kind of book: full of hope, packed with power."

—STEVEN FURTICK, lead pastor, Elevation Church and *New York Times* best-selling author of *Crash the Chatterbox, Greater,* and *Sun Stand Still*

"*Good Things* will train your eyes to see God, his goodness, and his favor upon you in every situation you find yourself in and will dramatically change your life. I so appreciate Kevin's solid approach and his uplifting voice."

—LYSA TERKEURST, *New York Times* best-selling author and president of Proverbs 31 Ministries

"In one of the most challenging seasons of my career, this phrase from Kevin Gerald got me through: 'This is just a chapter—it's not the story.' Kevin has been a leader in my life for the past ten years, through the ups and downs, and he has been there challenging me to keep my perspective right. With this book, I'm confident he can encourage and challenge you to see God's goodness in your life more clearly."

—JONATHAN STEWART, NFL running back, Carolina Panthers

"With inspired biblical insight, Kevin Gerald challenges us to look deeper in our understanding of what God's favor is all about. The result is like putting on a new pair of glasses and realizing what you've been missing.

Loaded with practical application for Christians in every season, *Good Things* will forever change the way you see the goodness of God and our abundant gifts as his children."

—CHRIS HODGES, senior pastor, Church of the Highlands
and author of *Fresh Air* and *Four Cups*

"With humor and truth, Kevin Gerald gives us the binoculars to see the limitless landscape of God's favor in a new and fresh way."

—MARK BATTERSON, *New York Times* best-selling author
of *The Circle Maker*

"Kevin's fresh approach to seeing God's hand in all circumstances of our lives is eye opening. His words craft a lens of awareness through which many will see God's favor with new clarity."

—DR. ED YOUNG, senior pastor, Second Baptist Church, Houston

"Seeing God's favor in your life can sometimes be difficult, especially if you are facing challenges, insecurities, or fears. Sometimes all it takes is a change in perspective. *Good Things* explains what God's favor is all about and how we can see it everywhere if we just look for it."

—CRAIG GROESCHEL, senior pastor of LifeChurch.tv and author
of *#Struggles: Following Jesus in a Selfie-Centered World*

"Kevin Gerald is a longtime friend and fellow church builder with a passion to see people experience a life of fullness and purpose. Read and be encouraged that despite life's many and varied challenges, the favor, mercy, grace, and blessing of our good and gracious God are both available and ongoing."

—BRIAN HOUSTON, senior pastor, Hillsong Church
and author of *Live, Love, Lead*

"In *Good Things,* pastor Kevin Gerald shows clearly that by walking in the favor and goodness of the Creator, your destiny will be directly impacted in a very meaningful way."

—Marcus D. Lamb, founder and president Daystar
Television Network

"The mirror of the Scriptures often reflects us rather than Christ, unless we have been prescribed the lens of favor. Kevin Gerald's book is your prescription!"

—Phil Munsey, chairman, Champions Network with
Joel Osteen Ministries

"I have personally been so blessed by Pastor Kevin's ability to see things from a perspective that clears through the distractions and brings new direction. His gift of making things that seem out of focus become clear is now accessible for so many through the pages of this brilliant book."

—Charlotte Gambill, author, speaker, and pastor of Life
Church in England with her husband, Steve

"A day of favor will change your life forever. I encourage you to read this book and share it with everyone you can: favor is just that amazing."

—Dr. Dave Martin, America's #1 Christian success coach
and author of *Another Shot*

"In *Good Things,* Kevin Gerald reminds us that God's favor and goodness aren't reserved for the superspiritual. The truth is that they are available to everyone, every moment of every day!"

—Ed Young, senior pastor of Fellowship Church and author
of *Outrageous, Contagious Joy*

"*Good Things* unpacks great insight on what true favor from God really is. Many people have a distorted view of God and his favor for our lives. This book will help change the mind-set that ensnares so many in bondage, never actually living the life God fully intended for them. *Good Things* will bring clarity to your life and renewal to your soul."

—LEE DOMINGUE, founder of Kingdom Builders U.S.,
     legacy pastor Church of the Highlands, and author
     of *Pearls of the King*

"Kevin Gerald is one of America's top communicators. As you read through *Good Things,* the unique wisdom he applies to a difficult topic will touch your heart and forever change your perception of God's favor."

—LEON FONTAINE, CEO of Miracle Channel and senior
     pastor of Springs Church

"In *Good Things,* Kevin Gerald does an amazing job of helping us see that when we know favor and walk in it, pride is depleted, and we are allowed to lead a life of humility, gratefulness, and generosity."

—SAM CHAND, leadership consultant and author
     of *Leadership Pain*

"*Good Things* compellingly challenges us to look for God's favor and goodness in our everyday existence."

—JENTEZEN FRANKLIN, senior pastor, Free Chapel
     and *New York Times* best-selling author

# Good Things

### Seeing Your Life
### Through the Lens
### *of God's Favor*

## KEVIN GERALD

### WATERBROOK
#### PRESS

Good Things
Published by WaterBrook Press
12265 Oracle Boulevard, Suite 200
Colorado Springs, Colorado 80921

Trade Paperback ISBN 978-1-60142-774-8
eBook ISBN 978-1-60142-775-5

Cover design by Kristopher K. Orr

Published in association with the literary agency of Fedd & Company Inc., PO Box 341973, Austin, TX 78734.

Published in the United States by WaterBrook Multnomah, an imprint of the Crown Publishing Group, a division of Penguin Random House LLC, New York.

WATERBROOK® and its deer colophon are registered trademarks of Penguin Random House LLC.

Library of Congress Cataloging-in-Publication Data
Gerald, Kevin.
   Good things : seeing your life through the lens of God's favor / Kevin Gerald.—First Edition.
      pages cm
   ISBN 978-1-60142-774-8—ISBN 978-1-60142-775-5 (electronic) 1. Grace (Theology) 2. God (Christianity)—Love. 3. God (Christianity)—Goodness. I. Title.
   BT761.3.G47 2015
   248.4—dc23
                                                 2015027962

Printed in the United States of America
2015—First Edition

10 9 8 7 6 5 4 3 2 1

*This book is dedicated to my dad, who is a steadfast and unwavering optimist. Thank you, Dad, for your stubborn insistence that God is good and would always do good things in and through my life.*

# Contents

## PART 5 • A LIFE OF GOOD THINGS

# Acknowledgments

S pecial thanks . . .

To Sheila, who is easily my best cheerleader.

To Jodi, the best contributor.

To Ryan, a constant encourager.

To Toni, for your strength in the details.

To Jen, the best project manager.

To Esther, my agent, who rekindled my fire to write again.

To Bruce, the editor extraordinaire.

To the film crew and focus groups and people who made them happen: Catalina, Andy, Paul, Nick, Scotty, Aaron, Robin, Nichole, Paula, Erik, Sue, and so many others!

To the #GoodFinders who join me on this mission.

# Beginning

His words were like waves of assurance as he spoke to the crowds gathered that day:

> If you then, who are evil, know how to give good gifts to your children, how much more will your Father who is in heaven give **good things** to those who ask him! (Matthew 7:11, ESV)

Have you ever wondered, as I have, what those good things really are that Jesus referred to . . . and why it seems some people receive more good in their lives than others?

Or maybe you have thought that good things are for everyone else but you . . . because you must have done something bad or wrong and are no longer on God's "good side"?

My main goal in this book is to convince you that you meet the criteria and have already been preapproved to experience a lifetime of good things!

I've found that many, if not most, of God's children don't experience all the benefits that come from being a member of *the* family. What's often missing is an understanding of an important concept called "favor." When we're unaware of the extent of God's favor, we're certain to limit it by comparing it to human kindness. When we do this we severely underestimate its unparalleled greatness. On the other hand, by elevating our awareness of favor we begin to experience immediate benefits and blessings.

I don't want to overpromise what you might gain from this book. But, seriously, this is information that can dramatically change your life . . . maybe even save your life.

Interested?

Let's go.

# Part 1

# God Is in the Good

# Am I Seeing Clearly?   (1)

I remain confident of this:
I will see the goodness of the LORD.

—PSALM 27:13

I can see clearly now, the rain is gone . . .

—JOHNNY NASH, A SONG
FROM THE '70S

I was standing in a beachfront sunglass store looking for a cleaning cloth to clean my glasses when the guy behind the counter said, "Here, try these on, turn around and look out at the water."

I'm thinking, *Can't the guy see that I've got sunglasses on?* So I said, "I'm actually just looking for a cleaning cloth . . ." He kept the glasses extended to me, "I can help you with that, but you won't believe these glasses . . . have a look while I grab the cloth."

A bit reluctant, I took off my glasses, put on the ones he'd handed me, and turned toward the ocean. It was an instantaneous "wow!" I was stunned. I was now seeing what I had not seen only moments before. There were vibrant colors and brilliant shades that seemed to shout, *I've been here all along waiting for you to notice me!* The view was nothing short of spectacular.

Forget the cleaning cloth! I bought my first pair of polarized sunglasses.

Since then I've learned how polarized glasses work. There are vertical lines and horizontal lines of light. The polarized lens eliminates the horizontal lines, which cuts out 100 percent of reflected light. This allows you to see what's behind or beyond the glare. For example, if you're on a boat you'll assume there are fish beneath the water's surface, but you don't actually see them due to the reflective glare of the sun.

> *There's a huge difference in assuming God is good and seeing evidence of his goodness.*

However, polarized glasses cut through the glare, and you actually see the illuminated life beneath the surface. The same is true when looking out across the horizon. The distortion is eliminated, allowing you to take in the full view beyond the glare.

Looking back I now know why the salesman in the sunglass hut continued to hold the glasses out toward me. He knew there was a clearer, brighter view.

My goal for this book is like that. I want to be like the guy in the sunglass shop, offering you a new, vibrant view of your life. Because . . .

*There's a huge difference in assuming God is good and seeing evidence of his goodness.*

And . . .

What if you could train your eyes to see the good? What if you could "cut through" the glaring issues of life and see God's constant presence and extravagant goodness?

## RANDOM BLINDNESS

Another time, I was standing at the sink in a public restroom washing my hands when a woman walked in. She looked confused, then horrified the moment she saw me.

To ease her embarrassment, I tried to lighten things by smiling big and saying, "Ma'am, you're in the wrong restroom." She quickly apologized, turned back around, and grabbed the door to leave. She was about halfway out when she suddenly looked back at me with a huge smile and said, "No, sir, you're in the wrong restroom!"

*Oh no!* Now it was my turn to be embarrassed and I made a quick exit!

Looking at the bold WOMEN sign out front, I asked myself, *How did I not see that sign?*

The reality is that **people don't see . . . what people don't see.**

Sometimes people wonder why they don't have faith or how they can have more faith. They may even pray for more faith. But what they don't realize is that faith is a product of our senses. The Bible says that "faith comes from hearing" (Romans 10:17). The reason faith increases from what we hear is that what we hear changes the focus of what we see.

When the things that you're hearing are negative, you will see the negative things in your life. It might be things your spouse, a neighbor, a person at work, or the nightly news is pointing out. Bad news comes from a lot of places. But regardless of the source, it will turn your focus toward what's wrong with the world and your life.

In the same way, when you hear good things from the people in your life or a positive program on the radio, your focus turns toward the good in the world. Your senses pick up what was less obvious before, and now you start to see what you did not see. Your sense of hearing has alerted your sense of vision, causing you to see what was hidden.

Cynics like to accuse optimists of not seeing or not being realistic about the negative realities of life.

I'm convinced it's just the opposite—that it's the positive reality that so often is blocked from a person's view. It's not that people don't want to see good things. They just can't see them! They have a distorted view of reality, one that is missing special moments and great blessings. When you don't see the whole picture, what you see is a distortion that can cause you to reach conclusions based on a partial view of your life.

One of the great deceptions of our time is the idea that "goodness" and "good things" exist on their own, without origin, aside and apart from God. Or worse, that goodness somehow originates in human beings. Practical goodness . . . common goodness . . . all goodness comes to be taken for granted.

All of this is a lie. The truth is that God is the source of all goodness and good things: "Every good thing given and every perfect gift is from above" (James 1:17, NASB).

However, when the lie is believed, then people dissociate good from God and often fail to see him as good. Not only that, those same people associate with God all that goes wrong in the world, which further obscures the truth that God is good and all good things come from him.

> God is the source
> of all goodness
> and good things.

When you separate good from God, you take away the awareness of God's goodness and mankind's need to thank, honor, revere, and worship him. The opposite happens when we connect good with God: we want to thank, honor, and worship him!

## LEARNING TO SEE

There's a story in the Old Testament where a servant of the prophet Elisha was seeing—with his physical eyes—all the opposition forces that were gathered against Israel in battle. But this man was completely unaware of what he could not see—all of God's protective forces surrounding them.

Elisha prayed that his servant's spiritual eyes would be opened so that he could see God's favor in the legions of angels that were protecting them in the middle of this high-pressure situation (see 2 Kings 6:17).

There's something that happens in our hearts and minds when we go from *hearing* that God is good to actually *seeing* God's goodness!

I can understand if you're wondering how a book called *Good Things* is going to offer a clearer, "polarized" view of life and how it can influence your life experience. It's actually kind of simple: *The more good we see, the more optimistic we will be.*

In life when I'm missing the good, it affects my outlook and even my spiritual equilibrium. Some days the good in life is obvious; on other days it hides itself in the routine, complexity, tragedy, and hardship of living. Back-to-back days of hidden goodness certainly can distort my view. They lower the level of my faith and can open the door to discouragement. All because of what I'm *not seeing.*

This distortion reminds me of the way my physical sight was before I put on those polarized sunglasses: *I didn't see . . . what I didn't see.*

# No More Turning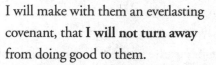

> I will make with them an everlasting
> covenant, that **I will not turn away**
> from doing good to them.
>
> —JEREMIAH 32:40, ESV,
> EMPHASIS ADDED

S o, before we go any further, let me ask you a question: What do you think God thinks about you?

I want an honest answer now—no need to try to impress me with a "religiously correct" answer like, "Well, he loves me."

That is the correct answer, by the way, but I'm after something a bit more nuanced.

I'm pushing here—I want the answer that comes out of your soul. What do you think God thinks about you?

There's no need to rush. I'm not timing how long it takes you to read this book.

Sit on it for a while. I'm not going anywhere.

*What do you think God thinks about you?*

• • •

I've been a pastor for a long time and an in-process human being even longer, and I've concluded that most of us—in the deepest reaches of who we are—don't really know the answer to that question.

If we're honest.

I think many of us believe that, in spite of what is clearly spelled out in his book, God is sort of waiting to see how we turn out before he totally decides what he thinks of us. We think to ourselves:

*"Some days I do pretty good."*
*"Some days I'm really bad."*
*"Some days are a mixture of both."*
*"I guess what God thinks of me kind of depends."*

The truth is that most people assume God's degree of approval of them is based on their behavior. So when they say the right thing and do the right thing, when they are patient with the kids or smile at the people who cut them off in traffic, God sees those things and turns on what I call the "favor faucet." So if they pile up enough of those good decisions and deeds, then the favor flow goes from a trickle to a fire hose in their lives!

On the other hand, they assume that when they provoke an argument with their husband, call in sick but spend the day on the golf course, or have a "man thought" about a woman other than their wife, God turns the handle down on the favor faucet.

Wrongly, people assume that God is constantly reacting to their *behavior* by approving or disapproving of them. The effect this has on people is that even when they are trying their best but still falling short, they think God is disappointed and pulling back his favor from them. It is a no-win situation. They already feel disappointed in themselves, and then on top of that, they imagine God's disapproval, which also probably means he's not interested in talking to them or helping them. And they assume God's favor faucet will stay off until they figure out how to get it on again.

These kinds of assumptions and imaginations are the termites of trust in our relationship with God. Rather than seeing God as a good God, we start to see him as a grumpy old man who seldom smiles and always has his arms folded. When actually God has his arms open, a big smile on his face, and he wants you to experience his kindness, goodness, and *favor.*

When most people hear the word "favor" associated with God, they assume that it's like a frequent flyer program that can be tapped into once you've logged enough miles on "faith and works" airlines. It's assumed that with enough miles you can earn the best seats, access to the travel lounge, and other favor perks. That's not how God's favor works.

> *Wrong assumptions are the termites of trust in our relationship with God.*

Using the airline analogy, God's favor is better understood by what happens when you're flying as a companion to someone who has earned the top status of a frequent flyer program and has passed along the benefits to you. It happens every day in airports around the world: People who are *not* frequent flyers can enjoy the spacious, exclusive airport lounge. They then bypass the long lines of people boarding the plane and sit in a first-class seat and enjoy a wonderful meal.

Again, these are people who have *not* earned the status or logged the miles. They don't *deserve* to be in first class, but they've been *invited* to be there. The status they are enjoying was given to them by someone who chose to transfer (by way of miles) to them the extra privileges. That's the nature of God's favor—it's always given, as an act of grace and kindness, by a God who has the desire and ability to give it; and it's a covenant God made to always do good and never stop doing good for his people. When it comes to God's people, his favor goes back to Old Testament times when writers described God's kindness and goodness toward them.

**I will make an everlasting covenant with them: I will never stop doing good to them.** (Jeremiah 32:40)

I will tell of the kindnesses of the LORD,
　　the deeds for which he is to be praised,
　　according to all the LORD has done for us—
yes, the many good things he has done for Israel,
　　according to his compassion and many kindnesses. (Isaiah 63:7)

God's grace expressed by his goodness may feel random or catch us by surprise, but from God's perspective, it's established in an everlasting covenant he has with humanity . . . *to never stop doing good to them.*

Plain and simple—**favor is promise based, not performance based.** It's based on God remembering a covenant he made in the past and acting on that covenant. He not only has the desire but the ability to show extravagant kindness. So that's what he does: he does good, and he never stops doing good.

> *The actual challenge for us is not gaining God's approval but rather accepting God's approval.*

The actual challenge for us is not *gaining* God's approval but rather *accepting* God's approval.

My goal in this chapter is to load you up with every reason why you can *stop seeking God's approval and start accepting God's favor.* To accomplish this, we need to do a little Bible study.

## I'VE HAD IT WITH THESE PEOPLE!

Even God seems to have his limits. There's no record of him saying exactly, "I've had it with these people," but the sentiment can be found. In the big picture view of ancient Bible history, it was common for God to turn away from his people. When they forgot who he was, neglected their worship of him, and turned to other gods, God turned away and withheld his favor. This typically led to seasons of hardship in their nation when enemies invaded, taking over entire cities and turning the residents into slaves.

God then sent prophets who preached and called the people to turn away from sin and other gods and turn toward the only true God. Men like Isaiah, Jeremiah, and Malachi called the nation back to God by preaching with word pictures of how God's favor would deliver them from their enemies, heal their land, and restore their wealth and properties. If the people repented of their sins, God would turn back to them and once more shower them with his mercy and favor.

The following sequence happened repeatedly throughout the Old Testament:

(a) In times of abundance and peace, God's people drifted spiritually and turned away from honoring God.

(b) God turned away from his people. The nation regressed in power and plummeted into physical and economic adversity.

(c) God reached out to his people through a prophet and promised favor in the form of restoration, healing, and economic stability—if they would turn back to him.

(d) The people responded to the message, repented, and turned back to God, and his favor turned back to them. The people then enjoyed seasons, even generations, of abundance and peace.

(e) But then the people drifted away from God and his ways and eventually returned to point A, and the cycle continued.

Even in good times there were still real-life challenges, such as bad weather conditions that affected crops and enemy nations that attacked.

However, the Lord's favor was on them. During the most difficult seasons, the people still experienced great blessing and an abundance of good things. Their economic strength gave them an advantage over their enemies, and they were able to establish themselves as a nation with a strong military presence and enjoy great peace.

At least until history repeated itself.

But then something happened that changed this pattern once and for all on God's end of things. It's as if he decided, *I'm not going to do this anymore. I've turned away when you've turned away, and I'm done with this. I've decided to stop turning.* Of course, God could have turned away permanently, but in his grace he chose to turn *toward us* permanently. No more turning away for God. No more withdrawing from man for seasons or periods of time. Man can still turn away from him, but God decided to never turn away from mankind again.

The key event in this divine adjustment, of course, came when God sent Jesus to earth as his expression of a once and for all turn toward humanity.

*This was the supreme moment in history . . . a very good thing.*

# The Best Year Ever ③

The Spirit of the Lord is on me,
because He has anointed me . . .
to proclaim the year of the Lord's favor.

—LUKE 4:18–19

The most obscene symbol in human
history is the Cross; yet in its ugliness it
remains the most eloquent testimony to
human dignity.

—R. C. SPROUL

One Sabbath morning Jesus went into the synagogue in his hometown of Nazareth and read a quotation from the prophet Isaiah that I believe clearly defined his mission and assignment on earth:

> The Spirit of the Lord is on me,
> because he has anointed me . . .
> to proclaim the year of the Lord's favor. (Luke 4:18–19)

*The year of the Lord's favor.*

What exactly did he mean?

Most success coaches recommend that if you want to succeed in life, you need a mission statement. They say that the more specific it is the better. Some say it should be so much a part of you that you even can say your mission statement when awakened in the middle of the night or at gunpoint when confronted by a mugger! The reason is that the clearer our mission is when we're under pressure, the greater our chance of success.

All good mission statements serve as an umbrella over a variety of related things we are seeking to accomplish.

Jesus had a few very specific things he came to do: he came to seek and save the lost, and he came to give abundant life. But when I think of his mission and the umbrella over it all, this statement Jesus made is the one big, inclusive but clear and very specific mission statement he made. Let's look at it again:

> The Spirit of the Lord is on me,
>> because he has anointed me . . .
>
> to proclaim the year of the Lord's favor.

In our culture today, Jesus's proclamation requires an explanation. *What's the year of the Lord's favor? Those are nice sounding words but what do they mean? And what does it have to do with God's favor on my life?*

The people who heard Jesus say that he had come to proclaim "the year of the Lord's favor" knew he was referencing the year of Jubilee—a special time on the Jewish calendar that came around every fifty years. In Bible times, the people who could not pay their bills would work as slaves for those to whom they owed money until their debt was paid off. Debt also often forced families to send their children as slaves to the people to whom they owed money. In other scenarios, the children stayed home, but their dad or mom went to work off the debt. Sometimes the debt was for unpaid government taxes, so those who owed money would have to go to debtors' prison. In all cases, families were separated.

But all of that changed in the year of Jubilee.

- Debt got canceled.
- Debt slaves and prisoners were freed.
- Land lost in foreclosures was returned to the original owners or their family.

You can see why the year of Jubilee caused a huge celebration. That's what Jesus used as his example when he spoke of the year of the Lord's favor.

## FAVOR IS NOW FIXED

When Jesus made his proclamation he wasn't referring to a particular calendar year, as we know it. He was referring to a new season, a new era in time, a new chapter in God's story of grace.

> *The cross is a symbol of God's never-ending, ongoing favor to all mankind.*

Jesus's proclamation was not directly about the event that the Jewish culture celebrated every fifty years. Jesus was using the year of Jubilee to reference his mission to earth. He was proclaiming that God's favor was coming on a whole new and greater level.

The year of Jubilee was a word picture that he used to convey an announcement of even greater hope. The old "on again, off again" relationship between God and his people was about to be replaced by a never-ending, ongoing commitment of God's favor to all mankind. And that new era in time began when Jesus spread his arms wide on a cross and made a permanent turn toward humanity.

On the popular NBC TV singing competition *The Voice*, contestants sing to gain the approval of the judges—some of the masters of pop music. When judges decide they approve of a person's talent, they hit the button that turns their chair and positions them face to face with the contestant. At that moment, instead of continuing an unbiased evaluation of the individual's talent, the judge immediately becomes an unabashed supporter committed to making the singer a success. By hitting the button and turning, the message is "I've heard enough! Now I want to go from being your judge to helping you be everything you can be!"

That's a picture of what it looked like when God turned his favor toward us. He made a decision. He hit the button. He turned in our direction and went from being a judge to approving of us and saying, "I'm for you! I am ready to help you be everything you are created to be!"

> *Don't worry about falling out of favor because of a failure!*

That "turn of the chair" happened over two thousand years ago when Jesus came into the world and, with one announcement, hit the button proclaiming what he called "the year of the Lord's favor."

I know this phrase—"the year of the Lord's favor"—may seem unfamiliar, but I promise it's worth your time to get a clear understanding of what Jesus was announcing.

"God so loved the world that he gave his one and only Son" (John 3:16)—that was God *turning* toward humanity, once and for all. When Christ died on Calvary, the perfect sacrifice was presented, making it possible for all who believe to enjoy God's favor. The great apostle Paul said it this way: "I tell you, now is the time of God's favor" (2 Corinthians 6:2).

So now every season is a season of favor!

God's favor is not on today and off tomorrow.

His favor isn't based on him being in a good mood.

Favor is not better at Christmas than Halloween.

God has chosen a position of endless blessing and ongoing favor, and there's nothing you or I do or don't do that changes that! God's favor is turned toward us and fixed on us. You don't have to wonder if God's for you! You don't have to worry about falling out of favor because of a failure!

*You are living in the time of the Lord's unending favor!*

## GIVE UP THE PREMISE AND STAND ON THE PROMISE

I hate to say it, but most people who claim to be "God's people" don't seem to really believe this "unending favor" business. Why would I say that?

It has to do, I believe, with a premise that seems deeply embedded in the core of every human being: we are invested in the idea that life is all about gaining approval. So when we are informed that we already have God's approval, everything in us fights against believing that. It's so counterintuitive, so not like the "real world" we live in.

It starts at a young age, usually, when we as children start recognizing the benefits of being accepted and approved of by all the "big" people around us. From then on we go after approval like a thirsty man goes after water. We may do it in different ways and for different reasons, but we all want approval. We are conditioned by life to seek approval, which means we live from the premise that we don't have it.

> *We are conditioned by life to seek approval, which means we live from the premise that we don't have it.*

Some people dress for approval, some play sports for approval, some people study hard for approval.

We try out for the team hoping for approval. We apply for acceptance into college hoping for approval. We seek out a job opportunity hoping for approval. We mix in with peers hoping for approval. We meet someone special and go the extra mile, mind our manners, brush our teeth, and comb our hair—hoping for approval.

But what if we *are* approved—by God of all people? That would make a big difference.

## THE FAVOR FAUCET

Snoqualmie Falls, which is just outside the Seattle area, is one of the most beautiful and impressive waterfalls in the world. The falls are 270 feet high, and 71 million gallons of water flow over the falls every minute.

My wife, Sheila, and I first visited the falls in the mid-1980s and have returned many times. One day while watching the endless flow of water, I thought about how the water I was watching come over the falls now had never come over the falls before. I thought about how every moment, every day, for all these years, fresh water has continued cascading over those falls. That's when I sensed God saying to me, *This is what my favor is like in your life . . . there's always a new supply flowing your way!*

The favor faucet is always turned on!

The fact is that God's favor

- is ongoing and never ending;
- never runs out;
- is always around us, on us, and with us;
- is not for only one season of our lives;
- is not something that is with us only when we've made the right choice or done the right thing;
- has no quota or measurement on it;
- is founded in grace; and
- is forever!

There's a Bible promise about God that squashes the approval premise. It goes like this: "For his anger lasts only a moment, but his favor lasts a lifetime" (Psalm 30:5).

I think most people have this promise backward: They see God's anger as lasting a lifetime and his favor lasting only a moment. They think God is unhappy and stewing under the surface at all times, like a grumpy grandpa whose anger has accumulated—that God's still upset at the world for things that happened thousands of years ago and still bothered by the things people did or didn't do in past generations . . . and are or aren't doing now!

Those who see God as stingy with favor consider themselves fortunate if they get brief experiences of his kindness and generosity in their lifetime. In their mind, God is usually irritated and disappointed in people. He stays that way except once in a while, when he forces a smile.

The truth is that God is way past old disappointments! He may have been angry about something you did or said, but he's

> The favor faucet is always turned on!

over it! Even if it happened earlier today, he's not resentful or agitated with your failure. When you have the image of an irritated, angry God stuck in your head, it automatically causes you to assume that your future supply of favor is very limited. As I was writing this chapter, the doorbell rang and the UPS man delivered a box to our house. I looked at the label just to make sure it was for us. Sure enough, it had our name and the right address. It's interesting how we sometimes wonder if God knows where we are in this vast universe. But if UPS can locate you and bring a specific package intended for you, then it seems completely reasonable that the God of the heavens has his own location-finding service on the job 24/7 and is able to bring you his blessings and goodness every moment of every day!

The good news is that God does know where you are and has an endless supply of favor he wants to deliver to you.

*God's favor is forever!*

Do not make the mistake of even subconsciously seeing God's favor as having seasons, quotas, terms, and conditions. No, instead I want you to remember the image of Snoqualmie Falls, minute by minute millions of gallons of fresh "favor" cascading into your life, in various seasons, in the daylight and at night, when it's cold and warm, when it's stormy and peaceful. There when you go to bed. There when you wake up.

The year of God's favor!

The very best year ever.

# No, Really, It's True (4)

Go, eat your food with gladness, and
drink your wine with a joyful heart, for
it is now that God favors what you do.

—ECCLESIASTES 9:7, NIV 1984

Are you convinced?

If you are like most people, this idea that God is on your side, has your back, wants only the best for you, is not watching your every move to give the thumbs-up or thumbs-down, and so on does not really stick without a bit more convincing.

So I'm here to tell you that it really is true—God is unconditionally committed to love you, support you, provide for you, and bless you. God is for you!

But let's discuss this some more.

• • •

I remember it like it was yesterday. I had wanted this so badly for so long! I had finally reached the ripe old age of sixteen, which meant I could take the test and get my driver's license. No more having to ask people to give me a ride; I would be able to go where I wanted, when I wanted.

I had taken driver's ed classes. I had studied my instruction book. I knew how to handle both the four-way and two-way stop. I had practiced parallel parking. I knew I needed the approval of that instructor before I would be allowed to drive.

As test day rolled around and I got behind the steering wheel, I kept telling myself, *Relax, don't get nervous and blow it.* Of course that's when all those anxious thoughts try to get in and mess you up: *What if I do blow it? What if the driving examiner doesn't like me? What if he is in a bad mood? What will I tell my friends?*

Talk about a first-world problem! I wanted that guy's approval that day more than anything in the world! And I knew that I had to perform well to get it. To mess up meant no approval, and no approval meant no driving. For me, at sixteen years old, there wasn't much that could be worse than that!

Approval is something we get if we perform properly, pass the test, get the grade, say the right thing, wear the right clothes, have the right job, or drive the right car. A lot of this is absolutely essential to a healthy and safe society. None of us want people to drive who haven't proven they are competent and ready to be behind the wheel. Nobody wants to board an airplane and hear that the pilot has never flown before. Imagine how fast people would be getting off that plane! What we experience in an approval-based society is not always a bad thing, but when that's all we know, it's almost impossible for us to not seek the approval of God. As you read this you might even be thinking, *But isn't that what we're supposed to do? Seek God's approval?* Remember, when you're seeking approval you're operating with the premise that you don't have it. But that's just the opposite of what God wants you to think about his approval. It's time to give up that premise and stand on his promise. He loaded up the Bible with words of love and affirmation to assure you that he approves of you! God doesn't want us to live in worry about gaining his favor. He wants us to rest in the assurance that we already have received his favor:

> Go, eat your food with gladness, and drink your wine with
> a joyful heart, for it is now that God favors what you do.
> (Ecclesiastes 9:7, NIV 1984)

This verse means we can live our lives with confidence and joy because we have God's favor. We don't have to get up every day and try to convince God to bless us. If you dread the thought of getting up in front of a group of people and performing, you are not alone. Millions of people suffer from performance anxiety, which is more commonly called "stage fright." In fact, most people would rather get the flu than perform. Athletes, musicians, actors, and public speakers often get performance anxiety. This is tragic because performance anxiety may prevent them from doing what they could otherwise do well and enjoy doing.

*Give up the premise and stand on his promise.*

As I'm writing this book, Aaron Lewis, the lead singer of the group Staind, flubbed a line of the national anthem before game five of the 2014 World Series. Lewis was barely two lines in before he sang, "What so proudly we hailed were so gallantly streaming" instead of "at the twilight's last gleaming." It turns out one of the more humiliating and interesting parts of the story was that Lewis had publicly criticized singer Christina Aguilera for making a few mistakes when she performed the national anthem at the Super Bowl in 2011. These are great examples of how even the best are more likely to fail when they feel performance anxiety.

So if you are getting up every day trying to be good enough to earn God's favor, you are only setting yourself up for failure. Try doing what the verse says to do: go and eat with gladness, drink with a joyful heart, *it is now that God favors what you do.*

Rather than performing for God's approval, live as if you already have it! Be confident that he has permanently turned his favor toward you. You are the apple of his eye! Thank him, sing to him, worship him. Go and eat with gladness. Drink with a joyful heart.

*God's favor is on you right now.*

## EVEN WHEN GOD DOESN'T APPROVE OF WHAT YOU'VE DONE, HE STILL APPROVES OF YOU!

In case you are wondering, I did pass my driver's test. It was a happy day when I was approved by the state of Missouri. To add to the joy, my dad rewarded me with a car to drive. Looking back I'm thinking maybe he and Mom were tired of being the taxi drivers, but whatever the reason, I was a driver and I had a car. It felt good. I felt like I was becoming a man.

But the real test came just a few weeks later when I wrecked the car. The worst part was that it was my fault. I remember being so nervous about my dad arriving at the scene. I had caused the accident and felt incredibly ashamed. How would he handle it?

We stood in the corner gas station looking at the damage. I knew there would be natural consequences. The car was messed up and other cars were damaged. Thankfully no one was hurt, but I felt so bad for what I had done. Honestly, at that moment I felt like I never wanted to drive again. I felt incompetent and undeserving to be out on the road.

But when my dad put his arm around me and said he was so glad that I was all right and that it would all be okay, I knew I still had his approval. He gave me no lecture. He didn't scold me or shame me. I knew I had messed up and would have some consequences to deal with. He seemed to know he didn't need to tell me that.

My dad was also the first to make sure I got back in the driver's seat. He knew I needed to do that instead of giving in to the voice in my head that was telling me I was a bad driver and didn't deserve to be on the road.

When my dad insisted that I drive the next day, I didn't interpret that as my dad approving of what I had done, but I did get encouragement that he still approved of me as a driver. He didn't say, *"I should never have let you get your license."* Or, *"I should never have got you that car."*

> *Nothing about the way he sees you changes. Nothing!*

He still believed in me. Although he didn't approve of what I had done, he did approve of me!

That's the way it is with God's approval of you. He's not surprised when you sin. He's not like, "What am I going to do now? You've blown it!" God's not surprised when you say the wrong thing and do the wrong thing. God's not caught off guard by your weakness, your goof-ups! But not only is he not surprised, try to lean in now and *hear* me say this: *Nothing about the way he sees you changes. Nothing!*

- Your status with God doesn't change.
- You don't go from being a saint to being a sinner.
- You still have your favor card.
- The gifts he gave you are still yours, and he doesn't regret giving them to you (see Romans 11:29).

Don't let yourself get down when you have failed to perform like you want to. If you hear words of condemnation, those words are not coming from God. Condemnation comes from your own disappointment in yourself, or from others, or from the Enemy himself. God's voice offers affirmation and approval.

His voice is the one telling you to get back behind the wheel and drive!

# Part 2

# The Origin of Favor

# Established in Grace (5)

or·i·gin, *n.* source; the thing from which
something develops, or the place where
it comes from.

I think this whole grace thing is pretty messed up. We throw the word
around, but do we truly grasp its significance?

We say grace before meals.

We talk about the grace with which someone navigates a situation or
a skater skates on the ice.

In church we sing and talk a lot about amazing grace.

And God's grace is awesomely amazing. But we still have messed
it up.

After twenty-five years of pastoring, I bumped into what I would call
the less proclaimed dynamics of grace. I may have just been the slow one
on this revelation, but it seems to me that grace has primarily been explained, elaborated on, written about, preached about, and talked about
as God's compassion and love that caused Jesus to take on himself the
sins of the world and nail them to the cross.

I know this message is typically what I referred to when I talked
about God's grace. And the truth is that this aspect of grace is so overwhelming and huge that we could spend our lives being incredibly grateful that God is not counting our sins against us—that he, in his mercy,
has forgiven, pardoned, and released us from the consequences we deserve as sinners.

It truly is an act of *scandalous* mercy that we, who are sinners, are now the righteousness of God!

The apostle Paul said it like this:

Like the rest, we were by nature deserving of wrath. But because of his great love for us, God, who is rich in mercy, made us alive with Christ even when we were dead in transgressions—it is by grace you have been saved. (Ephesians 2:3–5)

In these verses Paul referred to the richness of God's mercy as an element of God's grace that has saved us from our sins. If that were the totality of God's grace expression to us, we wouldn't complain. In fact, I think we tend to be so overwhelmed by the richness of his mercy that we hesitate to say there's more.

> Favor is the outworking of God's grace.

But there is more! It's called favor. Favor is the outworking of God's grace. Its origin is in the same grace by which we receive salvation. Which means favor, like salvation, is undeserved and is something to be received, not negotiated or bartered for.

Mercy is like a judge finding you guilty but then withholding any punishment. Favor is like the same judge then awarding you $10 million and making you his beneficiary after finding you guilty!

Favor is getting something you could never have imagined—an inexplicable gift. It's already too good to be true that we're pardoned from the consequences of sin. But now we're also the recipients of an ongoing, extreme, extravagant, unreasonable, over-the-top expression of kindness?

I like to think of mercy and favor as two trees growing in the garden of God's grace. The mercy tree gives us everything we need to stand shameless and approved by God. The favor tree adds the unimaginable goodness of God to our everyday lives.

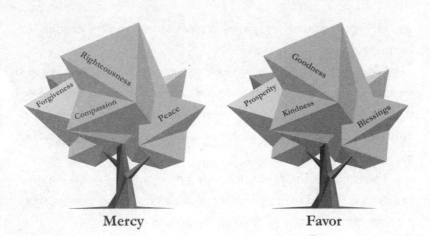

Mercy                                          Favor

Chances are high that when you read the practical implications of the outworking of God's grace, you will be tempted to dumb down the extravagance of God's favor. That's what we were mulling over earlier with all the premise talk. The reasoning might sound like this in your head: *Kevin, it's gonna take the rest of my life and all of eternity to thank him that I don't get what I deserve . . . and then you want me to start trying to get my head around the idea that God wants my life experience to be so much better than I deserve?*

If that's how you feel, I understand. I too am amazed at God's extravagant favor. But that is exactly what I'm asking you to wrap your head around.

Brennan Manning said this: "My deepest awareness of myself is that I am deeply loved by Jesus Christ and I have done nothing to earn it or deserve it."[1]

## GOD DOES US A BIG FAVOR

One of the best pictures of this is the parable Jesus told of the prodigal son. In the story the son is a thrill-seeking, fast-living, bad-decision-making guy. He lives impulsively and goes after pleasure, only to lose everything he has in the process.

When he comes back home seeking mercy, the father goes beyond mercy and shows an abundance of favor to the undeserving son, showering him with expensive gifts and throwing a party in his honor. And rather than shaming him, he celebrates and affirms him. He declares how happy he is to have him home.

This father of the prodigal is a picture of our God. God not only grants *mercy* to the undeserving but he is also ready and eager to show *favor* on the undeserving.

> God's mercy doesn't give us what we deserve. God's favor gives us what we don't deserve.

Favor doesn't do a background check or consider a person's history. It doesn't put people through a screening process. God's favor doesn't do an evaluation and ask you to qualify. The reason so many people struggle with this is that undeserved mercy is hard enough to accept—much less undeserved favor on top of it. But that's how good God is. His plan is not just to save us from sin; he wants us to have an abundant and blessed life!

Talk about *good things*!

Think about it this way: when someone says to you, "I want to do you a favor," what he really is saying is, "I want to do something for you not based on something you did to deserve it. I don't expect you to pay me for it. I just want to do you a favor."

God's all over that.

Simply put, God's mercy is why those of us who trust in him *don't get what we deserve* as sinners. Through mercy, God stepped in and gave us a pardon from the deserved consequences of our sins.

Favor, on the other hand, is why believers *get what we don't deserve* in the form of God's abounding and endless goodness on our lives.

You can think of it like this: *God's mercy doesn't give us what we deserve. God's favor gives us what we don't deserve.*

## FAVOR ISN'T FAIR BECAUSE LIFE ISN'T FAIR

One of my favorite movies is *The Blind Side,* the story of a white family who brought Michael Oher, an African American homeless teenager, into their home. They gave him a bed, food, a family to be a part of and, most of all, a hope for his future. This family's love and support helped bring out the best in Michael, who went to college on a football scholarship and has played professional football for the Baltimore Ravens and Tennessee Titans.

When the movie starts you can't help but feel sorry for Michael. He didn't deserve to struggle so much in his early life. As the plot progresses it becomes glaringly obvious that the only way the story could have a happy ending is if Michael gets some huge breaks. There's no way that the undeserved rejection he experienced early in life could be overcome without undeserved acceptance.

That's exactly what happened.

He gets extravagant love and acceptance from an unlikely place. He needed it and he got it. An unusual, extraordinary favor. An open door. A huge opportunity. This is why we all have to be open and eager to receive God's favor.

We need the favor of God in order to get beyond our sin nature. We were born sinners. We didn't have any chance of not being a sinner. It was an unfair start because we didn't choose to be a sinner. There's no way that the undeserved sin could be overcome without an undeserved gift of righteousness.

That's exactly what happened. That's what continues to happen.

Scripture says, "My God will supply all your needs" (Philippians

4:19, NASB). Make sure you don't define your needs as being what you have to have to barely get by. That's not how God defines needs. God defines our needs as being everything we need to live an abundant, overcoming, and prosperous life. Everything we need to overcome poverty and inadequacy. Everything we need to take care of our families, send our children to college, and give generously.

Define your needs from the perspective that your Father in heaven has an endless supply that he wants to provide you with. God's not hung up on whether it's fair or whether you deserve it—so make sure *you* don't get hung up on it! Just welcome his blessings, knowing that he is committed to taking care of you.

> Grace is the unmerited favor of God.

When you see favor as an expression of God's grace, you start to notice favor happening to you that's disproportionate to what you deserve. You'll start recognizing that God through his own nature desires to bless you. The more you see God like this, the more you will start to see God answering your prayers and opening doors for you.

Favor isn't fair, so don't try to make it fair!

When God blesses you, don't apologize or try to legitimize God's blessings to people who may be jealous of you. When others are blessed and you feel they don't deserve it, you're probably right! Just don't resent undeserved favor in their lives if you're going to welcome it in yours!

Remember, favor can't be fair because life isn't fair. The unfair, undeserved, random distribution of favor is the response of a just God to an unfair world.

It's the unmerited favor of God.

• • •

I heard the story of a man who dies and goes to heaven and, of course, Peter meets him at the pearly gates. "Here's how it works," Peter says.

"You need one hundred points to make it into heaven. You tell me all the good things you've done, and I give you a certain number of points for each item, depending on how good it was. When you reach one hundred points, you get in."

"Okay," the man says, "I was married to the same woman for fifty years and never cheated on her, even in my heart."

"That's wonderful," says St. Peter. "That's worth three points!"

"Three points?" the guy says, sounding a little disappointed. "Well, I attended church all my life and supported its ministry with my tithes and service."

"Terrific!" says St. Peter. "That's certainly worth two points."

"Two points? Golly. How about this: I started a soup kitchen in my city and worked in a shelter for homeless veterans."

"Fantastic, that's good for one more point," he says.

*"One point!"* the man cries. "At this rate the only way I will get into heaven is by the grace of God!"

"Come on in!"

That pretty well sums it up.

# What About Mondays?  ⑥

You have allowed me to suffer much
hardship,
    but you will restore me to life again.

—PSALM 71:20, NLT

Everything we see hides another thing;
we always want to see what is hidden by
what we see.

—RENE MAGRITTE

Can you relate to this?

In my experience, about the time I'm really buying into a great truth like "the favor of God," I have *a Monday,* and my enthusiasm rushes out like air from a pricked balloon.

Actually, one time I had a Monday on a Sunday.

Sundays are almost always a terrific spiritual high for me . . . I'm a pastor! So why on a Sunday afternoon was I at Sea-Tac Airport feeling the urge to leap over the ticket counter, grab the ticket agent by the throat, and strangle him with his own striped airline tie? This does not sound like something a pastor should be contemplating.

Less than an hour before, I had finished speaking my message and hurriedly walked, almost ran, off the platform after incredible services at our church. In a pastor's world, we typically start the week off thinking about the *next weekend.* We pray, plan, and prepare all week for the weekend. Then on Sunday morning all this bottled up energy peaks with excitement as people around us experience God's presence and we proclaim God's promises. When Sundays go well, I typically sense and see God's favor all around me.

But evidently the ticket agent hadn't gotten the memo. I had left the service in a rush because I was scheduled to speak in another city that night. My personal assistant had everything planned to expedite time, including having already picked up a sandwich for me at Subway so I could head straight to the airport and then have something to eat on the plane.

So now I was at the airport with my carry-on and the Subway sandwich bag sitting on the counter when everything went into s-l-o-w motion! The ticket agent moved even slower than normal and seemed annoyed with me as I tried to hurry him along with good-natured comments about how I really needed to catch that plane and was "cutting it pretty close."

Finally, after an unnecessarily long and drawn-out process, he handed me my ticket and with a smirk said, "I suggest next time you're in a hurry to catch a plane that you not stop and pick up a Subway sandwich on your way to the airport."

Grrrrrr! That's the moment when all the favor I had felt from a Sunday suddenly switched off and Monday began. The plummet from feeling high and happy to low and angry happened faster than on a speeding roller coaster at Six Flags.

One minute, favor; the next, frustration. This is a snapshot of what God's favor sometimes looks like in a faulty world.

Indulge me for a philosophic moment. *Metaphorically there are only two days a week: there's Sunday when God's favor is obvious, and there's Monday when God's favor feels absent.*

On Sundays it's like heaven is open and blessings are pouring out with my name on every one, and on Mondays it feels like heaven has lost my address. On Sundays I feel like I'm the apple of God's eye, and on Mondays I can feel like the discarded core. On Sundays I think if it gets any better I'm going to implode, and on Mondays I think if it gets any worse I'm going to explode.

> *The path of favor is not always on the mountaintop; it also winds through the valley.*

Something tells me that this is not just my experience. I think everyone who has experienced the loving gaze of God on a Sunday has also experienced the feeling that they couldn't seem to get even a glance from God on a Monday.

Monday is usually not about a major crisis but often the accumulation of smaller disappointments:

- the unexpected overdraft on our bank account
- the denial letter for the college application
- the disconnect in our communication with our spouse
- the growing discontentment in our job
- the son or daughter struggling in school

These kinds of disappointments may not qualify as major crises, but they can certainly create prolonged, ongoing, back-to-back Mondays.

Maybe one of the most helpful things I can tell you about a lifetime of favor is that it doesn't exempt you from the ups and downs of life. The path of favor is not always on the mountaintop; it also winds through the valley.

Hopefully, you're already realizing that my explanation of God's favor is not a denial of Mondays. Neither can I offer a formula for eliminating the Mondays. What I am hoping to do is to help you see and experience more of God's goodness in the Mondays of your life. It's understanding that *Sunday's favor doesn't stop with Monday's challenges.*

## SAVING THE FUTURE

*Maybe this book will save you from too much Monday.*

Before you conclude that's an arrogant statement made by an author wanna-be-savior, let me explain what I mean: Have you downgraded your expectations of God's favor because of life's hardships? Maybe on the outside you're keeping it together, but on the inside your hopes and dreams are barely alive.

There are many reasons why life starts looking a whole lot more like Monday than Sunday, but all of them can be summarized by your existence in a faulty world. Day in and day out it's taken a toll on you to the point where now maybe even your future seems in jeopardy—not your *existence* but your *future*. The one you hoped for. The one God planned for you.

The reason I know that some people need their future saved is because there was a time when I desperately needed my future saved. It was in that season when this book was born. This book didn't originate in a protected bubble of blessing that I've decided to share with the world. It began when the lights started fading in the bright room called my life and reduced my perspective to what I could see by flickering candlelight.

I was a youth pastor just getting started in ministry when I experienced an avalanche of up-close and personal tragedies. Six different people, all of them in my inner circle of life, experienced untimely deaths. Some suffered greatly. Some deaths were completely unexpected and sudden. All were in the prime of their lives. Looking back I remember hitting every emotion on all eight cylinders.

I questioned everything I had believed about God answering prayer, bringing justice, and being good. None of it felt right. None of it made sense. None of it was fair. Outwardly, I tried to keep my game face on, but inwardly my world was rocked. In addition, I was being sought out by others to offer some sensible, reasonable explanation of what was happening in this fairly small, close-knit group of believers.

Hungry for explanations and reeling in pain, I watched some people emotionally and spiritually lose their footing. I watched people around me curse the heavens, some sob for days uncontrollably, while others retreated into isolation. The truth is, at points I either did or thought about doing all the same things.

> *God's undeserved goodness is not just equal to hardship; it is surpassing in greatness.*

My questions outnumbered my answers by at least four to one. Much of what I had believed about God seemed invalidated. The residue that remained on me when the dust settled was a new sense of uncertainty. My confidence in God was downgraded and my expectations of life were moderate at best.

It was on the heels of that emotional and spiritual fight, as I continued to try to move forward, that I first met Sheila. The timing was not coincidental. My melancholy personality had stooped to an all-time low and along came this good-looking, spunky, fun-loving, high-energy person who knocked melancholy me off my feet!

After meeting her it was like the clouds rolled back and the sun came out! I knew I didn't want to do life without her. It was in that season after we married that I encountered God's goodness not just experientially but theologically.

*But I still have Mondays.* Days when I want to punch out some smirking airline ticket agent.

I know better now, though, that even if the goodness of God does not *cancel* the pain of life's hardship, the goodness of his favor *exceeds* the pain of life's hardship. As the psalmist wrote,

God's undeserved goodness is not just equal to the undeserved hardship. It is surpassing in greatness. (See Psalm 71:20–21, NLT)

The favor of God means there's a good future.
Sunday always comes.

# Heaven's Nepotism  (7)

I will be a Father to you,
    and you will be my sons and
daughters, says the Lord Almighty.

—2 CORINTHIANS 6:18

The Lord's prayer calls for this affirmation: God is my Father! I am his child!
I am somebody! I bear his honorable
name!

—ROBERT SCHULLER

O kay, I get it. That's probably not the wisest choice for a winning chapter title!

*Nepotism* is a word that exits our mouth under a dark cloud. It's not a nice word. How could I ever somehow connect it to the righteous, generous nature of God?

Have I lost it?

No, actually, I'm only stating the facts. He—*God*—really has this "thing" about his kids.

In our everyday interactions with people, we all want equal opportunity. We want an even playing field, where the people who make decisions are unbiased. If we interview for a job, we want the person making the decision to do so purely on the skills needed to do the job. Nothing smacks of bias more than status given that's not *earned*. A promotion given because of a relationship offends our sense of fair play.

But here's the deal: God's favor on us *is unearned*. It's based purely on *relationship and identity with God*. Much like parental favor, God's favor is natural and relational. Parents are supposed to favor their children, and children are supposed to experience the favor of their parents.

The definition of *nepotism* is "favoritism shown to relatives; favoritism shown by somebody in power." I can't imagine anything that better describes the basis of God's favor on us. It is favor that's flowing our way as sons and daughters of God.

Children are supposed to know that if they are in a crowded day care, when their parent comes through the door he or she will be looking for them. That *my dad's eyes* will search past all others to *find me* and take me home with him. It's the validation and identity of knowing who I am and to whom I belong that affirms a child and sets a child up with confidence and assurance in life. It's a good thing for a child to sense early on that *my parents will always be here for me*.

> God saw you and blessed you before you showed up on the earth.

In the same way, God wants us to know that about him. It's why Scripture declares God will never leave us nor forsake us (see Deuteronomy 31:6; Hebrews 13:5). When God says he will be a Father to you, he's providing the surest evidence of his never-ending, ongoing favor in your life. He wants you to know that your origin is in him. That you're not here by accident or coincidence but by divine design. God saw you and blessed you before you showed up on the earth. God formed you and created you in his image. You are a recipient of his favor and blessing.

Jesus explained a parent's desire to bless his children as being similar but much milder in nature than God's desire to do good for those who pray to him and look to him as their source:

> If you then, who are evil, know how to give good gifts to your children, how much more will your Father who is in heaven give good things to those who ask him! (Matthew 7:11, esv)

What Jesus was saying is that God's favor flows as naturally into our lives as a father's favor flows into the lives of his children.

A father's favor naturally provides (no begging or appealing is necessary).

A father's favor sees the possibilities and potential.

A father's favor creates opportunities and opens doors.

A father's favor means he wants the best for his children.

## Favor Is Not Based on *Who* We Are
## but on *Whose* We Are

I am blessed to have the world's greatest dad. My dad's good name and reputation have given me favor that continues to this day. That favor was especially potent in St. Louis, the city where I grew up.

When I was about twelve years old, I remember Dad introducing me to the then vice president of our local bank and opening up a savings account in my name. The banker's name was Frank Ziegler. I remember standing nervously in front of Mr. Ziegler's desk as my dad said, "Frank, I'd like you to meet my son. This is my son Kevin. We are opening his first account today, and I'd like you to help him like you've helped me."

Mr. Ziegler and I had many conversations over the next decade where he advised me and helped me establish and manage my first savings and checking accounts. On several occasions he went out of his way for me. When I needed assistance he was there for me, helping me make good decisions while buying cars and starting a small business.

To this day I'm grateful, but I also realize that what Mr. Ziegler did for me was, in large part, based on who my father was. In fact, what I found out later was that my father had signed papers as a "backer" on my accounts. If I had a shortfall of income versus withdrawals, my dad had agreed to cover me. I benefited from my father's status with the bank. It was what he had in his accounts, his good name, and his reputation that qualified me.

Although I was nervous that first day as I sat in front of Mr. Ziegler, those types of experiences speak to the heart of a son or daughter: *You are noticed. You matter. You are loved. You're my child, and I'm your father.*

Parenting is about a lot of things: instruction, discipline, and protection to name a few. But nothing is more vital and God-like when it comes to parenting than a huge dose of affirmation, especially when it's unearned, detached from any kind of affirmation based solely on performance.

## THE NEW NEPOTISM

The name "Trump" is everywhere. It's on resorts, office buildings, golf courses, condominiums, and entertainment centers.

Trump is a growing financial empire that began back in the 1930s when Fred Trump, the son of German immigrants, launched into his career in real-estate development. When Fred died in 1999, he left the majority of his fortune of $400 million to his children. Those children have had children, and the empire has continued to grow from generation to generation. Now worth billions, the fortune is being inherited by a new generation of the Trump family.

In Adam Bellow's book *In Praise of Nepotism,* he presents a "new nepotism" as a positive contrast to what he calls the old nepotism.

According to Bellow, the old nepotism meant parents provided opportunity for their children, which they didn't deserve and, even more importantly, did not choose. It involved a prearranged, predetermined future, which was decided by the parents for the children.

The result of this old form of nepotism was that many of the children of wealthy parents undervalued their inheritance. Their parents had servants and employees working hard in the family business, and the children who were heirs were often indifferent and ungrateful. Under this form of nepotism, families passed their estates on to children who wasted what their parents had paid a great price for. Rather than stewarding their blessings, the heirs squandered them.

> Heaven's nepotism
> is an opportunity
> given to us based
> on our choosing it.

Now contrast that with what Bellow calls the "new nepotism," where children are still recipients of their family fortune, but they receive it by *choosing* to follow in their parents' footsteps and steward the opportunities given them as heirs to the family fortune.

In kind of the same way—and long before anyone wrote a book about the new nepotism—heaven came up with a plan of blessing and favor for God's sons and daughters. In what we call the old covenant or Old Testament, which was something like the old nepotism, God promised blessings on Abraham's seed. In love he imposed his favor on the nation of Israel. He declared them heirs of his goodness and promised they would be favored throughout all generations.

Through time God saw that his favor wasn't always welcomed and wanted, as new generations of Israelites undervalued the favor they were born into. This is when God said, *I'm going to open my favor up to all people. I'm going to adopt sons and daughters out of every tribe and nation. I'll still be a God who favors his sons and daughters, but under the new covenant my family favor is for those who* choose *it.*

Heaven's nepotism still seems a bit scandalous and is unearned, but under the new covenant it's received by choosing to follow Christ and steward the opportunities given to us as members of God's family. It's fully realized and experienced when it's acted on.

Heaven's nepotism is something to be *chosen*. It's an *opportunity given to us,* but it is *conveyed to us based on our choosing it.*

## OUR TREE OF FAMILY FAVOR

Family favor is an advantage no matter how you look at it. When people say "blood is thicker than water," they are referencing the reality that family, by nature, has a favor advantage others don't have.

Because God thinks in terms of family, Scripture repeatedly traces for us believers our own history as Christ followers back to our father of the faith, Abraham. Here's why that's important: God declared his blessings and favor over Abraham and his descendants for all time. He made it clear that Abraham's children throughout all generations would experience favor from heaven, and they also would bless nations. In Christ, we are children of Abraham and heirs of that promise.

Here is one of the clearest scriptures of family ties between modern Christians and Abraham:

> And now that you belong to Christ, you are the true children of Abraham. You are his heirs, and God's promise to Abraham belongs to you. (Galatians 3:29, NLT)

Who wouldn't want to be in Abe's clan? Who wouldn't want to be included in the family? There's no doubt if you are in Abraham's "down line" that you have the favor advantage, an opportunity to experience a covenant of blessing with Abraham and his descendants.

You certainly can choose words other than *nepotism* to describe what's going on in "our family." We definitely are enjoying favors we kids never earned or deserved. But let's not feel bad about all this, because our Dad has left the door open for anyone else who wants to get in on a very *good thing.*

# Abraham's Heirs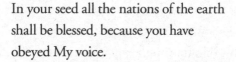

In your seed all the nations of the earth
shall be blessed, because you have
obeyed My voice.

—GENESIS 22:18, NASB

I want to add a few more insights about our great-great-great (add as
many more greats as you like) grandfather Abraham.

Now that we understand how great it is to be one of his descendants,
it's important to know what it means to be an authentic Hebrew.

*Say what?*

I'll explain. All modern thought originates from two foundational
philosophies. One is rooted in Greek concepts and thinking, which is
where the majority of popular worldviews comes from. This would be
known as Western thinking.

The other philosophy is Hebrew or Eastern philosophy, which origi-
nated with the ancient Hebrews who were the children of Abraham and
are spiritual ancestors of today's Christians. The Bible, both Old and
New Testaments, was written by Hebrews from a Hebrew perspective.
(Even though the New Testament was written in Greek, the authors had
a Hebrew education and background.)

The Greek mind-set is very different from the Hebrew mind-set in
its views of God. When the Greek mind reads the Bible it can completely miss or dismiss what the Hebrew mind intended to convey, and

perhaps the greatest thing missed by the Greek mind is the intention of Scripture to show how God wants to convey favor and blessing on his people.

In this chapter, I want us to take a look at several statements that represent important aspects of the Hebrew mind-set. And, hopefully, by taking a look at some of these concepts we can realize what our legacy is more clearly—how our ancestors of the faith thought—so that we too can adopt this thinking and apply it to our everyday lives. It may seem foreign to us and even contradict what is popular in our society today, but this is God's way of thinking, and it can become ours as well:

- The ancient Hebrews saw God as a God of blessing and themselves as God's blessed people.
- The ancient Hebrews viewed God as a very practical and relevant God.
- The ancient Hebrews saw God everywhere in everything.
- The ancient Hebrews had a holistic, integrated approach to life.
- The ancient Hebrews assumed that God's blessing meant holistic success.
- The ancient Hebrews saw God's blessing on them as means through which the world would be blessed.

## A PRACTICAL GOD

### 1. The ancient Hebrews saw God as a God of blessing and themselves as God's blessed people.

The Hebrew word for "blessing" is *barakah*. It appears in Scripture over seven hundred times, and it means "to be given power to succeed, to prosper, and to leave a legacy." The Amplified Bible describes *blessed* as "happy, fortunate, . . . and enviable" (Psalm 1:1).

In addition, the word *prosperity* is found ninety-two times in Scripture and is, as a rule, associated with what happens to those who experience God's blessings.

The book by Bruce Wilkinson, *The Prayer of Jabez*, has helped a lot of people by giving them permission to pray what Jabez (an ancient Hebrew) prayed when he cried out, "Bless me indeed, and enlarge my territory" (1 Chronicles 4:10, NKJV).

> *God wants us to pray for our financial needs with the same ease that we pray for our food.*

I've heard people on occasion say, "Money is not important to me." What most of them mean is, "There are things more important to me than extra money," since, in reality, money is extremely important to all of us. Money is why we work forty-plus hours a week! If money is not important, then why go to work?

If you have no money,

- you have no food, clothing, or place to live;
- you have to borrow, beg, or steal to survive, and
- you can't help anyone else; you have nothing to give.

You see, money is important. The Bible says money answers all things (see Ecclesiastes 10:19), which means that all of our natural needs like food, housing, and transportation are met by us having enough money. God wants us to pray for our financial needs with the same ease with which we pray blessing on our food, health, and family.

If God didn't want us to be comfortable talking about money and praying for financial stability, there's no way he would have mentioned money-related topics so often in Scripture. There are approximately two thousand scriptures on financial-related topics. It is the thing that can buy you food and land. Money pays for a place to live, builds churches, funds outreach and missions, and builds hospitals and universities. Money supports God's kingdom on the planet and blesses the world!

## 2. The ancient Hebrews viewed God as a very practical and relevant God.

Now contrast that with the Greek mind-set that views God as more mysterious, mystical, abstract, distant, and uninvolved. For example, the Greeks saw God as a "God above the clouds." The Hebrews saw God as a "God beneath the clouds."

A Greek description of God would be "God is love," which *describes God in relation to God.* This keeps God *mysterious,* in heaven and unengaged in man's everyday life. A Hebrew description would be "God loves me," which *describes God in relationship to myself.* This view personalizes God's goodness and brings God out of heaven and into our everyday lives.

The Old Testament descriptions of God as our provider, healer, shepherd, and peace all come from the Hebrew view that personalized God and focused on who God is *to us.*

## 3. The ancient Hebrews saw God everywhere in everything.

The Greek mind saw God at church and everything else in life as secular. Hebrew thinking says all that is good comes from God, making all things sacred.

For example, technology is something a Hebrew mind-set would thank God for and believe God gave to us and would want used for good. Both education and medicine would be viewed in the same way—gifts from God to be used for good ends. So, also, money is something a Hebrew mind-set would see as a blessing from God, thank God for it, and be comfortable having a lot of it to use for good.

The Greek mind-set, which separates God from what is going on "beneath the clouds," tends, therefore, to see all human inventions, brilliance, skill, and labor as separate from God. Two things can happen as a result of this mind-set:

First, people can get filled with pride assuming that what *they do* is done without God's help—*It's my talent or it's my skill or it's my hard work that got me where I am.*

Second, the Greek mind-set not only takes credit for all of its success but also sees God as disinterested in success. Seeing God as disinterested sounds like, *I don't ask God for help in practical things because he's much too busy for that. If I did that he would be insulted. I'm just an insignificant blip on the radar screen of God's mind because he has much more important things to worry about in keeping the cosmos together!*

People who think like this listen to a preacher like myself tell people that God is good and wants to do good things for them, and they often become uncomfortable . . . even mad. They think we're just getting people's hopes up with some sort of magical, medicine-man, hyped-up jargon. They think this way because that's the way the Greek mind responds to a message of God's hope and promises in our lives today.

The reality is that as Christians, we are part of Abraham's family who walk in the hope and live in the promises of God—just as our father Abraham did.


## LIFE'S PRIORITIES

*4. The ancient Hebrews had a holistic, integrated approach to life.* On the other hand, it's common for the Greek mind-set to strive to compartmentalize life. I remember as a kid at church camp listening to a youth leader as he tried to help us prioritize what's important in life. He suggested we make a list something like this:

- God first
- Family second
- Others third
- Church fourth
- Self last

He meant well, and for a long time I saw this as the right approach to life. Then it started getting more obvious that it wasn't always that cut-and-dried, that the items on my list of "what was important" could not be put in somewhat direct opposition to one another. I started to realize in that way of thinking that something important had to lose for something else that was important to win. It really wasn't God versus family, or family versus church. It was actually all of the above working together as allies, not adversaries.

In the world of computers and their hard drives there's something called *defragging*. It's short for *defragment*. What happens is that hard drives store information in "blocks" or "files," and fragmentation happens when those blocks or files get separated and are far away from each other. Rather than making the computer more efficient, the separation of information actually slows down the computer and makes it operate less efficiently.

So defragmentation is the process of pulling it all together, which makes a computer more effective.

One common tendency of people is to view life that is not compartmentalized as being out of control. They may imagine that their lives are more productive and easier when every part is in more-manageable separate files and folders. The truth is just the opposite. Our lives are more efficient when we pull our nonnegotiable values together. **A compartmentalized life may offer more control but less capacity.**

I know this may sound odd and a bit counterintuitive to the very organized person, but it's a simplification of our life priorities, where they each strengthen one another with no energy wasted by opposing one another.

Choices in life get easier and make more sense when we make this shift and take a holistic, integrated approach to success in life. When we put God in the center, and love family, love people, love the church, and love ourselves, we can see how it is all intended to be integrated and mutually enhancing.

This is why Jesus said, "Love your neighbor as yourself" (Matthew 22:39). He didn't say love your neighbor *not* yourself. So many people neglect themselves rather than take care of themselves, because they have a list and self is at the bottom of the list, which means there's never any time left for "me." Eventually, their family life suffers, their marriage suffers, and/or their health suffers. They self-implode because they have failed to think holistically about success in life, which is the ancient Hebrew approach to life.

## THE BLESSED LIFE

### 5. *The ancient Hebrews assumed that God's blessing meant holistic success.*

Blessed in the city and in the field, blessed at home, blessed in business, blessed in relationships, blessed in family, blessed in finances—that equals holistic success (see Deuteronomy 28).

The ancient Hebrews saw their work and business as an opportunity to honor God.

The Hebrew word for "work" and "worship" is the same word—*avodah,* which explains the Hebrew view of the unity and wholeness of life. In the Hebrew mind, one's work is as much an expression to God of worship as one's worship through singing and praising God. After all, Scripture does say, "Whatever you do, work at it with all your heart, as working for the Lord" (Colossians 3:23).

> *God gives humans the opportunity to work as a way of including us in his creative process.*

Because of the influence of the ancient Greek mind-set, many Christians see work as the necessary thing they have to do to survive in life because of Adam and Eve's sin in the garden. What people don't realize is that work existed before the Fall. Adam had a job given to him by God to manage and take care of the garden God had put him in.

God gives humans the opportunity to work as a way of including us in his creative process. What the Greek mind calls secular, the Hebrew mind sees as a blessing given by God. To learn a skill or a trade; to build, plan, develop, and solve problems and needs; and to expand, heal, educate, provide a service, and leave a legacy—the Hebrew mind sees all of these as opportunities to honor God.

**6. The ancient Hebrews saw God's blessings on them as means through which the world would be blessed.**

They saw God's blessings of abundance and wealth not as taking resources from others but as a means to bless and enrich people in need.

In Genesis 12 God said to Abraham,

> I will bless you;
> I will make your name great,

and you will be a blessing. . . .
All peoples on earth
will be blessed through you. (verses 2–3, NIV 1984)

This is still true today. The more we are blessed, the more opportunity we have to be a blessing, which is exactly what God wants from us! His hope is that the blessings he gives us will overflow into the world around us and that all nations would be blessed through us.

# Part 3

# A Better Lens

# Good Eyes

Faith demonstrates to the eye of the
mind the reality of those things that
cannot be discerned by the eye of the
body.

—MATTHEW HENRY
ON HEBREWS 11:1

Seeing is of course very much a matter
of verbalization. Unless I call my
attention to what passes before my eyes,
I simply won't see it.

—ANNIE DILLARD

Early one morning in Washington DC, a man quietly took his place against a Metro wall, pulled out his violin, placed his "tip hat" on the ground, and began to play. For this day he had chosen six selections from Bach. During his performance, over a thousand people walked by. While passing by, some slowed their pace, others stopped to listen briefly, and a few dropped some sympathy money into the hat.

Unknown to everyone who passed, the "beggar" on the street that morning was the world-renowned violinist Joshua Bell. The instrument that sang in his hands was a violin valued at $3.5 million. When Joshua finished, there was no applause, no standing ovation, nothing to acknowledge the magnificent talent that had just been on display. And his street concert netted a mere thirty-two bucks. Just forty-eight hours earlier, an eager crowd had packed a Boston theater to hear him, paying an average of one hundred dollars per seat.

How could anyone miss this? The master violinist did a charity concert and over a thousand people walked by without noticing? How does that happen?

The fact is that the people who passed by that day represent a trait common to all of us: we don't always *see* what's right in front of us. But the fact that we don't see it doesn't mean it's not there.

Just what's wrong with our eyes, anyway?

## BAD EYES—GOOD EYES

Jesus told us, "The lamp of the body is the eye. Therefore, when your eye is good, your whole body also is full of light. But when your eye is bad, your body also is full of darkness" (Luke 11:34, NKJV).

> *The only thing that's different between a negative person and a positive person is what they "see."*

My eyesight is not as poor as some people's. But when I have my glasses on I can read with a lot more ease and catch details that I otherwise miss. Just as people go to an eye doctor to get glasses or have surgery to give them better eyesight, we're not stuck with our current life paradigm. We can choose a better one!

The word *paradigm* comes from the Greek and is, in a general sense, a reference to a set pattern or way we see the world—not in terms of our physical eyes but in terms of our assumptions, beliefs, and overall perspective. It's what we might call our mind's eye.

This is what Jesus was referring to as he explained the eye as the lamp of the body. He was saying that the eye can be good or the eye can be bad, and the condition of our eye affects what we see or don't see, what we experience or miss out on. If our eyes are good, it's like turning on a lamp inside of us. We brighten up in our spirits because we're living with a greater awareness of God's goodness and blessings in our lives.

The opposite is true about bad eyes; they miss seeing the good. They may or may not take in darkness, but they definitely don't take in light. What they don't see is not what they are incapable of seeing but typically what they are not trained to see.

In a similar way, the only thing that's different between a negative person and a positive person is what they "see." Two people can grow up in the same home with similar life experiences, and one will be negative about life and the other will be positive. Even though they have been surrounded by the same environment and have the same parents, what they see and the way they see it is different.

Negative people are not bad. Pessimistic people are not ignorant. In fact, oftentimes negativity is a trait of people who are highly informed in what they call reality. When passing along their perspective, they will tell you, "I'm not being negative; I'm just being real!" And they are being real in what they are aware of and educated in, which is the "life is hard" reality. They have taken pages of notes and have the data to support the fact that life is not a gravy train!

When people are deeply educated in the "life is hard" reality but undereducated in the "God is good" reality, they lean toward the unfavorable possibility versus seeing the possibility of something good. The reason these persons can get stuck in their negativity is that they have accepted that the "life is hard" reality cancels out the "God is good" reality.

I've found that anyone, even people highly aware of the "life is hard" reality, will become authentically optimistic when they educate themselves in the "God is good" reality. You don't have to deny the realities associated with life being hard to see the realities associated with God being good! (Later in chapter 12 we're going to talk more about the "life is hard" versus "God is good" view of life.)

## SELECTIVE SEEING

My wife, Sheila, will tell you that she's often amazed at what I don't see. Or what I don't notice! I can walk right past something without realizing it. It could be the trash bag in the kitchen that needs to be taken to the garage. Or the unmade bed. Or that note she left right on the counter where I couldn't miss it. I always feel ridiculous when I don't see what seemed impossible not to see! Not only that, but I also feel hard pressed to explain to Sheila that I'm not intentionally missing what she wants me to see! When this happens, I find myself explaining, appealing, maybe even borderline begging her to believe me—"I'm being honest . . . I'm telling the truth . . . I really did not see it!"

Maybe this issue is genetic. My mom used to tell how my dad did not see things right in front of him. A particular story happened when I was about three years old. Mom and Dad were shopping separately in a large shopping center. My dad came up to my mom, and when he realized I wasn't with her, with a worried look he asked, "Where's Kevin?" She burst out laughing so hard that she couldn't answer him, which only upset him more, because I had fallen asleep and he was carrying me! So there I was, literally lying on his shoulder! Because his mind had been distracted, he'd forgotten I was right there!

Maybe I did get my seeing challenges from my dad—like father like son!

So, again, what we don't see is not necessarily what we are incapable of seeing. It's more often what we're not thinking about, looking for, or trained to see.

In the same way we don't see some things, there are other things we can't seem to miss.

I grew up in St. Louis and to this day I'm a devoted Cardinals baseball fan. Living in Seattle and traveling around the country, I'm amazed by how many Cardinals hats and jerseys I see on people in places other than St. Louis. Of course Cardinals emblems are everywhere in St. Louis, but I see them many other places too. The truth is, most people wouldn't even notice a Cardinals hat in Minneapolis or Tampa, but since my mind's eye is trained to notice the Cardinals logo, without any effort I spot it in a crowd, walking through a mall, and on an airplane.

> *All of us can see less of what we don't want to see and more of what we become intentional about seeing.*

I think years ago when I was just a kid, a little scribe in my head made a mental note that read something like this: "Kevin is a Cardinals fan. Kevin watches baseball, plays baseball, buys baseball cards, and talks about baseball with his friends. Kevin's favorite baseball team is the Cardinals. He pretends he is on the Cardinals team. He loves wearing Cardinals jerseys and hats. So help him see Cardinals baseball cards, hats, and jerseys. Point them out to him because he loves the Cardinals!"

So even now, years later, it's like my mind is on a mission to show me Cardinals stuff.

In the same way I see Cardinals logos and gear, everyone's eyes are trained to see what their mind has assumed they want to see. So while I'm Cardinals minded, someone else is boat minded or fishing minded or music minded or tech minded. Some people are fashion minded or art minded or sports minded.

Something can be all around us and we do not see it, while there are other things most people don't notice but our eyes don't miss.

I have some encouragement for you: all of us have the potential to see less of what we don't want to see and more of what we become intentional about seeing.

## YOUR INTERNAL SCRIBE

The reason behind all this selective seeing is a small part of our brain called the reticular activating system (RAS). I'm definitely not an expert on this, but those who are tell us that God created our mind to notice what it thinks we want to see and store it for easy retrieval. In its attempt to do this, it will bypass tons of information and focus on what it thinks we want to see and remember.

In the same way a computer remembers the words you've entered and websites you've visited so it can retrieve information for you quickly, your mind helps you see what you want to see and overlook what you don't want to see. It's like having a little scribe in your mind that's making a mental note of what it thinks you want to see more of and then eagerly pointing it out to you.

This "record-keeping scribe" does this by filtering for the relevant information and presenting it to your conscious mind, helping you recall it. Your brain continues then to collect more information that is relevant to that specific goal. It takes pride in efficiently showing you what you want to see.

Think about it: the last time you wanted something (a specific car, tennis shoes, smart phone, hairdo, or even to lose weight), the moment you made that item or topic your focus of attention, it seemed you were bombarded with advertisements about it. If you were interested in a specific car, all of a sudden you noticed the car everywhere; if it was tennis shoes, you started noticing those shoes on other people's feet. If your interest was to lose weight, your RAS filtered information relating to the latest diets, and you paid more attention when other people talked about losing weight. This information had always been there, but you now were seeing more of it.

I'm sure we have all experienced this phenomenon to some extent, because the little scribe in our head is taking good notes and doing his best to point out to us what he thinks we want to see.

Years ago when the actress Drew Barrymore was filming the movie *E.T.*, she started what she calls a lifelong love affair with hearts, a passion she later channeled into photography. Barrymore sees heart-shaped objects or images everywhere and photographs them. She sees heart shapes in places where nobody else sees them—in man-made objects and in nature.

The little scribe in her mind has picked up the fact that *Drew loves hearts . . . Drew wants to see hearts . . .* The scribe works hard every minute of every day to locate hearts that Barrymore can see and take pictures of. (Eventually, Barrymore included the pictures in a book called *Find It in Everything*.)

However, there's a dark side to this little scribe—it can become a *culprit*. Like everything God gives us that is intended to help us, there usually is a downside. The little scribe can work against us by pointing out what it would be better to not notice or pay attention to. When this happens, the only thing we can do is be intentional about reprogramming our RAS to tell us what *we want* to see, not what *it thinks* we want to see.

A common example of this is when we change an address or phone number. Our brain has the former information stored in autopilot; as soon as we need to retrieve our address, the brain happily offers it up quickly. But when we move, our brain doesn't automatically switch over to the new information until we get intentional and override the old stored file and replace it with the new.

A few years ago our family moved to a new address, and one day shortly after moving, I left the office and drove to where I used to live. I pulled in the driveway, got out of my car, and walked all the way to the front door before I realized I didn't live there anymore! Awkward!

My brain was on autopilot and took me exactly where it thought I wanted to go. Once I rerouted my brain to see "home" as a different location, it worked to memorize and record the way to my new address.

The scribe can be stubborn in its assumption that it knows what you want more than you do, but it will eagerly enter new data and reprogram once it is sure you really want the new data stored. This rerouting, *retraining*, reprogramming potential of our mind is not just to help us find our house after we've moved but, more critically, to help us see more evidence of God's blessings and favor in our lives!

## ENLIGHTENED EYES

When the apostle Paul wrote to the believers in the city of Ephesus, he told them he was praying that the "eyes of [their] heart may be enlightened" (Ephesians 1:18). God's goodness isn't hidden, and neither is God's favor making limited appearances in our lives. Remember what the psalmist said: "Your favor surrounds me" (see Psalm 5:12). So we know it's there. But that doesn't mean we're aware of it, which is why Paul prayed for his friends to be enlightened.

> *God's goodness isn't hidden, and neither is God's favor making limited appearances in our lives.*

To be enlightened means to become aware of something for yourself that others may already know and may even have tried to show you. You didn't see it for whatever reason until you became enlightened.

One of the things Sheila and I sometimes do on vacation is walk through art studios and admire various paintings and pieces. It's an amazing experience when the owner of the studio takes a piece of art to an enclosed space and lets you see the painting lit properly. The brilliance of the artist's work can be appreciated only when the lighting is right. What looked like an average picture now takes on an incredible multifaceted beauty that is stunning!

Sheila and I are not well versed in art, but on more than one occasion we either had to leave quickly or get our checkbook out because the picture was so compelling! It wasn't a different picture, but we were seeing it in a new light.

Once you see God's favor more clearly, the intentionality becomes hard-wired into the searching mechanism of your daily life, causing you to see it like Drew Barrymore sees hearts.

A prayer to see more of God's unseen goodness is definitely a prayer worth praying.

# What You Get Is ⑩
# What You See

Keep your face to the sunshine and you
cannot see a shadow.

—HELEN KELLER

Most of us have heard the cliché, "What you see is what you get."
I'm choosing to rearrange the words to reemphasize the truth
about our eyes. "What you get is what you see," which is why we want to
*choose* what we *see*, so that we can *get* what we *want*!

Sheila and I were on vacation in Hawaii sitting by a pool when a man
who was reading his paper nearby started filling me in on all the things
he saw wrong with the world. Every few minutes I tried to redirect the
conversation to where we were, the incredible view of the ocean, and the
near-perfect surroundings of Hawaii. But every time I did that he wanted
to take the conversation back to all the world's negative news and obvious
troubles and problems.

*Oh boy, what do you do?*

As I listened to his nonstop complaints about politicians who were
screwing things up and the coming economic disaster about to take our
country down, all I could think was, *How can I save this rare, much-
anticipated day in Hawaii? How do I protect the grandeur of this morning from what feels like a party-crashing, people-bashing assault on my
fun in the sun? Somebody help me!*

But the reality was that it wasn't just my day in Hawaii; it was also his day in Hawaii. He and I were both surrounded by the same beauty, the same atmosphere, and the same opportunity.

But our reality was different.

Two people can be in the same exact place in life and be living from two different realities. They are sharing the same experience but seeing two totally different things.

At times, I too have been that guy obsessed with the reality of a faulty world. It is pretty messed up! I've done my own share of focusing on what's wrong and what's unfair and what doesn't make sense. But that's not who I want to be moving forward. And I'm thinking that maybe you don't either.

Cognitive distortions are simple ways our mind convinces us of things that are not really true. For example,

- *We see one side and not the other.* We tell ourselves that we're being rational and accurate, but in reality we're not seeing the whole picture.
- *We overgeneralize.* If something bad happens in one area of our life, we now think life is bad in general and start to expect more bad things to happen. That's bad!
- *We think in black-and-white terms.* If you think you and your life have to be perfect or you're a failure, that is "either/or" thinking that doesn't allow room for opposing realities, which is the nature of reality!

These are just a few examples of how cognitive distortions occur and distort our view, causing us to reach inaccurate conclusions.

But what if that could change? What if there's a sort of polarized lens that would eliminate the distortion and help a person to see "good things" they previously missed?

What if this could happen for you? What if you could see past the distortions caused by a faulty world and clearly see God's favor for you?

What if you were able to always see the blessings in greater proportion than the problems?

How different would your outlook on life be?

How would your relationships be impacted?

How much easier would it be to remain confident in crisis?

I'm not suggesting there's nothing wrong in the world. I don't want to turn away from the very real and urgent needs around me, but I want to see more of God's goodness. I want to focus more on what's right about God rather than what's wrong with the world—not just for my sake but for the sake of those around me. If I have a firm hold on God's goodness, then I have something to offer the people in my airspace. If I'm saturated in the awareness of God's extravagant grace and favor, then I'll be a messenger of God's hope to the world.

## GOD'S AT WORK

When you start looking for good things, you realize they are sometimes found in unlikely places. In fact, when God's goodness is least visible it might be functioning at its highest and best on our behalf.

> *When you start looking for good things, you realize they are sometimes found in unlikely places.*

For example, do you remember the story of Joseph? Talk about life not going right! Joseph was betrayed by his brothers, sold into Egypt as a slave, falsely accused of adultery, and thrown in prison. Meanwhile, God strategically was moving him into position to be the most powerful leader of the land, second only to pharaoh! Scripture says Joseph was experiencing favor in the struggle (see Genesis 50:20). Not just before the struggle or after the struggle but in the middle of the struggle!

When we don't get the job we wanted or the person we were dating breaks up with us, we're often quick to assume God's favor has vanished. But then in time we come to realize that God was actually doing us a favor. Maybe he saved us from hardship and struggle in that job we wanted or from being seriously hurt in that relationship. Maybe God had a better job and more fulfilling relationship in mind! This is where faith in God's favor is essential if we are going to experience all he has for us.

Even though sometimes an incident or a season in our life causes distortion and lacks clarity, we must remember that God is working toward something good in our life. **It's favor not yet visible, hidden by a process that can be painful.** Sometimes we assume God is not at work when we are in the middle of a bitter-tasting experience. The truth

> *No matter what your perspective on life, you're not stuck with it.*

is, like with many food spices and ingredients, some experiences won't taste good until they get mixed into the recipe of God's plan for our lives.

It's only then that we realize with greater confidence that it's all worked together for our good. Our role is to trust God in these seasons when his goodness is invisible and to believe we have God's favor even when there's no evidence to support it.

Favor surrounds us. It's in front, behind, above, and on both sides of us. The psalmist said, "Surely, LORD, you bless the righteous; you surround them with your favor as with a shield" (Psalm 5:12).

So, no matter what your perspective on life, you're not stuck with it. We all have God-given potential to change our perspective, to change where we put our focus. To embrace a new and better outlook on our circumstances. To start seeing the blessings and the favor that surround us.

## ADJUSTED PERSPECTIVE

One day a woman in our church shared with me that she was weary in her marriage, and if her husband didn't change, she just couldn't take any more. I knew her husband and had considered him a good man, husband, and father.

As I listened to her describe all her frustrations, I found myself waiting for her to get to the "big thing" that had pushed her over the line and would justify her readiness to walk away from the relationship. What I was hearing were the somewhat common sources of frustration and challenges between two people who have different personalities and approaches to life. (This is probably a good time to say how common this is in marriage—opposites first attract, then attack!)

Finally, when I realized that I had heard everything the weary and discouraged wife found wrong with her husband, I asked her to do me a favor: "Tell me what is good about your husband?"

After a few moments of consideration she answered, "He's a good dad—our kids absolutely adore their father!" I waited, and then she said something else that was positive about her husband. After she named three or four more things I said, "Here's what I want you to do: write those things down." I handed her paper and pen and she started writing. Then I asked her to take the list home and every day find and write down at least one more good thing about her husband.

I saw this lady again only a few days later and she was smiling. She thanked me and laughed at herself for having gotten so wrapped up and absorbed in what was wrong with her husband, rather than seeing all that was right about him. Now, years later, she and her husband are still members of our church. She has said many times that she has looked back and been so glad that she changed her perspective about her marriage. I'm sure she's had to repeat that exercise over the years, because we all slip into focusing too much on the wrong things. But the great thing is seeing how well she and her husband have done, as well as their children and grandchildren.

There are tremendous rewards that we may never experience if we don't train our eyes to see the good.

## EYE TRAINING

I grew up in the Midwest, and one of the favorite things the guys in our family did was hunt. My dad owned a beautiful Labrador retriever who was a prize-winning bird dog. We would sometimes allow other hunters to bring their younger dogs to hunt with Dad's dog so they could learn from him. The frustrating thing about those younger, inexperienced dogs was that they had not learned to differentiate the scent of other game from that of quail. So when we took the younger dogs hunting, we had to watch them run off chasing rabbits, squirrel, or deer. They didn't know yet that what they wanted to show us was not what we wanted to see.

When the younger dogs started running off, their owners would look at our Labrador, and if she wasn't headed that same way, they would call their dogs back, correct them, and keep them following the dog trained to find the quail.

The trained bird dog knew what to look for. It was always fun to see our Labrador "go on point." When she would get a few feet away from birds hiding in tall grass, she would freeze with

> *Training your eyes to see the good means training the scribe in your mind to hunt for the good.*

her nose pointed straight in the direction of the birds. Again, she certainly must have noticed other scents just like the younger dogs, but she stayed committed to finding and pointing out what she knew we wanted to see.

Training your eyes to see the good means training the scribe in your mind to hunt for the good. That will take some patience and determination on your part, but if you stay persistent, it's well worth your investment of energy.

If it's your desire to see more of God's goodness in your everyday life, you gain an incredible advantage when your RAS knows to stop and point out the evidence of his goodness. When your RAS knows that's the goal, it starts looking for blessings and favor like my little mind scribe hunts for Cardinals caps and jerseys. Or like a trained bird dog looks for quail. We each have a beautiful mind designed, ready, and willing to show us more of the good that comes directly from the God who is good.

"Bad eyes" are often bad because of perspectives we've picked up from other people:

- people in our family
- people we work with
- people we go to school with
- people we listen to on the radio or watch on television

Our brain assumes that what we listen to or hear other people say is how we want to see the world. It records other people's perspectives and then draws from that to form our opinions and views. Without realizing it, we form a perspective that becomes our ideas . . . about God, church, people, work, relationships, and everything else in life. It's the way we see things, and our brain keeps hunting for more data of what it guesses we want to see to build our case for that outlook.

One of the essentials to seeing God's unseen goodness is to get your RAS hanging out with people who hunt for goodness and find it more often than you do. There are "good finders" all around you who are well trained in looking for and finding the good. The people you've currently surrounded yourself with may not have good eyes, so it may take a little effort to develop connections with some good finders. But I assure you they are around—at school, church, and work. They can let you in on their reading materials, media interests, whom they follow on social media, the music they listen to, and all the other habits that serve them in being finders of good things.

One key to making this effort count is to remember that you're there to learn how to find what *they* see, not teach them to find what you see. When people who are steeped in the "life is hard" perspective try to convert people who are educated in the "God is good" perspective, it usually doesn't work because the "God is good" people are already aware that life is hard! If they keep hearing from you that "life is hard," eventually they will stop hanging out with you. They are the *good finders* and they want to continue to be. They are like the hunting dog passing up other scents that will take them off course because they have trained their eyes to search for quail—the good things!

> *Good is synonymous with God.*

Everything has its pluses and minuses—every relationship, every job, and even every church, which means there's a bright side to everything. If I look for it and see it, I then begin to draw and attract light into my life. (Remember Matthew 6:22: "The eye is the lamp.") So what I attract or draw into my life is not just what's around me but what I *see* when I look around me. It's not a coincidence that Jesus said that good eyes come before a good life (see also Luke 11:34).

Some people think their eyes are bad because their life is bad, and they are convinced that if their life was good then their eyes would be good. Such people are waiting for their circumstances to improve so they can have a better outlook on life. But according to Jesus, the perspective comes first . . . then the circumstances improve.

What I've discovered is that there are tremendous benefits to seeing the good.

As I've mentioned before, good is synonymous with God.

I'm not talking about what feels good or appears good—sometimes we think something is good only to find out it just seemed good at the time—I'm referring to what is actually good.

When I see good I see God.

My faith increases.

My confidence stays strong.

I'm happier.

I'm easier to get along with.

I face life with an upbeat attitude.

Simply put, *the more good I see, the more optimistic I am.* I believe that's also true for you.

# A Favor-Friendly Mind ⓘⓘ

Men do not attract that which they
want, but that which they are.

—JAMES ALLEN

For as he thinks within himself, so he is.

—PROVERBS 23:7, NASB

Although the favor of God is impartial from one person to the next, it simply is not compatible with everyone's attitudes and mind-sets. In other words, the attitudes and mind-sets of some people keep God's favor at a distance, while the attitudes and mind-sets of others draw it in.

Wherefore gird up the loins of your mind, be sober, and hope
to the end for the *grace* [charis] that is to be brought unto you.
(1 Peter 1:13, KJV)

This word *charis* comes from the Greek *xáris* and from the Hebrew word *kaná,* which is a reference to God's grace expressed through his favor and kindness toward us. But it has an even deeper connotation: *charis* describes God *reaching (inclining)* to people because he is *ready* to bless them.

A visual image of *charis* pictures God leaning in, eagerly extending himself to show his favor to us. The apostle Peter, the author of this verse, is telling us to rein in our thought life so we're not distracted or drawn into speculations and fears but we remain hopeful, expecting to experience God's favor at all times. He's saying that we should stay mindful (keep your mind full) of favor so we can experience the fullness of favor that is "to be brought unto you." There is favor that is coming our way! We should remind ourselves, *Don't blow it . . . Don't let your mind mess it up . . . Heaven has some awesome things planned for you!*

When you have the right mind-set you become favor friendly. You'll think in ways that cause favor to be drawn into your life and be part of your life. Nothing increases favor in our lives like thinking favor and expecting favor.

I'm not into gimmicks, so I'm absolutely certain that no amount of crafty mind games will trigger an avalanche of God's goodness in my life. What I have found, though, is overwhelming evidence that I experience more favor when I think more about favor.

This idea that we've talked about of seeing more of God's goodness is the basis for becoming what I call favor minded. Being favor minded means you have hope . . . you live with expectation of the best. You have a confidence in God and believe that he is for you and with you, and that he is working all things for your good.

> *Nothing increases favor in our lives like thinking favor and expecting favor.*

Nobody is favor minded every moment of every day, but being favor minded means you're intentionally doing what the Bible refers to when it tells you that you can be transformed by the "renewing of your mind" (Romans 12:2).

For centuries renewing the mind was mostly a biblical concept that wasn't supported by science. During most of the twentieth century, the consensus among neuroscientists was that brain structure was fixed and didn't change after early childhood. Since then, however, scientists started changing their opinions and created a term—*neuroplasticity*—that is defined as "the brain's ability *to reorganize* itself by forming new neural connections throughout life."

What God has known since the beginning, science is now discovering: no matter what our age, we have the ability to *change the habits of our mind.*

Research shows that how we think repeatedly does literally create small pathways or "grooves" on our brains. With some intentional effort, we can redirect our habits of thought and create new grooves or pathways in our brains. It takes time and effort, but it is the key to transformation.

For example, you may have heard it takes twenty-one days to form a new habit. The reason for this is it takes about that much concentrated time for our new thoughts to build a new path to travel on. In other words, this is what the Bible refers to as the renewing of the mind.

One reason for this renewing of the mind is so that we will think in a way that is congruent with having faith in God. If someone hasn't been thinking about God's favor, blessings, and promises, new thought patterns will not be set overnight. However, by being deliberate, the mind will adapt quickly to a new way of thinking—becoming favor friendly.

Another way to better understand how our minds work is to compare the function of our minds to the search engines of a computer. Search engines are software programs that probe the World Wide Web looking for the keywords we've requested.

In the same way, your mind has a search engine that is constantly seeking what we tell it to look for—consciously or subconsciously. Since the human brain produces about seventy thousand thoughts on an average day (which is about one thought every 1.2 seconds), our brain is searching even when we don't know it's searching. It's constantly going "out there" and "pulling in" data based on the primary tendencies and leanings of our minds. So here's what this will look like:

- *If you are trouble minded, you will find trouble everywhere.* The trouble minded will notice trouble before there is actual trouble. They will see trouble coming, and it will come in predictable waves.
- *If you are anger minded, you will have reasons to be angry when nobody else sees a reason to be angry.* In this mind-set, a person will become angry over incidents that other people around them don't even notice.
- *If you are problem minded, you will find problems with every solution.* In this mind-set, there's always a problem, and every problem leads to another problem. When you're trying to help problem-minded people by offering solutions, they just find more and more problems.
- *If you are poverty minded, you will always see yourself as lacking and poor.* Poverty-minded people never see themselves as being rich. The poverty inside draws in a lifestyle of poverty. They give less than they can give and fail to enjoy what they have because the poverty in them makes them live poor.
- *When you are favor minded, you will find more favor.* Being favor minded won't remove the daily challenges, but it will point you toward favor and more favor.

You can be aware of trouble—but *think* favor!

You can be aware of problems—but *think* favor!

You can be aware of setbacks—but *think* favor!

Think favor so you can open up the search engine in your mind for favor. Turn your mind toward favor and watch how favor data starts to appear—*evidence* of favor. *Reasons* for favor. An avalanche of ongoing favor that comes by consistently *thinking favor*!

## FAVOR WILL BE BROUGHT TO YOU

Chances are this new thinking about favor won't come naturally to you. It doesn't come naturally to me either. Sometimes I can sense my own thoughts going downhill faster than a runaway sled on an icy slope. If you're like me, this is all the more reason to not allow your mind to be drawn away from the confidence and assurance of favor *to be brought to you.*

Even as you're reading this now, perhaps there are things going on in your life that cause you worry or fear. Maybe there are problems at work or home. Maybe there are pressing financial concerns. It would be easy to imagine the worst and be terrified. But maybe what would be better is to imagine the worst and be confident and assured that no matter what happens there is *favor to be brought to you.* I'm not suggesting we give up awareness of the worst possible scenario, but I am saying that we have to face our worries and fears with assurance and confidence. When we stay favor minded, we can expect a positive outcome no matter what happens!

Two business owners in our church, Dan and Tammy, are great examples of staying favor minded through all kinds of situations and circumstances. They will be the first to tell you that their journey has had many challenges, but they have known God's favor along the way.

Dan and Tammy did not inherit a business or prepare themselves early in life by getting their business degrees. Nothing quite like that! Dan was an alcoholic who had lost his first wife and son due to complications at the end of her pregnancy. After that tragedy he moved to Washington State where he met and married Tammy. Shortly thereafter, Dan got saved and they began attending church together. Both were working in the retail trade and collected cardboard on their way home to recycle and sell in order to pay their tithe or save some money for a future business.

One day they asked if I would pray with them about a contract offer they were about to make to buy a gas station. Holding that contract in our hands, we prayed together asking God's blessing on their business. And since that day we've repeated that prayer several times together as their business has grown and they have purchased different properties.

One piece of land they purchased was intended for a second gas station. They had a lot of opposition with one man in the city during the construction phase, and when it came time, they could not get their occupancy permit.

One day as Dan sat on the curb by the property, discouraged and having a pity party, he asked God, "Why?" Dan felt like God answered by telling him to go again to that man who had opposed their permit, to humble himself, and simply tell the man that he had no hard feelings toward him.

Dan walked into the office and the man was startled to see him. Dan apologized to the man if he had dishonored him in any way and asked his forgiveness. He told him he was a Christian and wanted to relieve any tension between them. Dan then turned and walked out of the office. As he was passing through the doorway, the man called out Dan's name and asked him to come back to see him the next day.

Dan returned the following day, and the man said he had never experienced anyone doing what Dan had done, then he handed him the occupancy permit. To this day Dan has a friend in a position of power who eagerly helps him with any city approval process. Dan and Tammy have been able to add more property to the gas station and expand their business to accommodate eighteen-wheelers.

As hard as it is sometimes to get in the right frame of mind, that's what has to happen for favor to be brought to you! Dan could have continued to be angry and frustrated about how he was being treated, and he would still be sitting on that curb crying. But when he picked himself up and left his own pity party, he created a place where favor could come into his life. He realized he couldn't stay angry with the people who opposed him and couldn't let the circumstances cause him to feel defeated.

When Dan started thinking at a higher level of grace and goodness, he experienced a flood of favor that continues to this day.

And by the way, as I write this book, Dan is celebrating eighteen years of sobriety too!

## YOUR MIND IS A MAGNET

When something enters the airspace of the earth, there's a magnetic force that pulls that object toward the earth. That pull of gravity is not visible but is undeniably and powerfully real.

In much the same way, what is in you is pulling something toward you. This gravity-like pull is generated by what's going on inside of you.

I heard the story of an old wise man who would sit alongside the road at the entrance to the city, greeting people as they would come and go. One family traveling into the city stopped and asked him what kind of people they would find living in the city. The wise man asked, "What kind of people were in the city you came from?"

"We didn't like it in the city we came from," they answered. "The people there were not very friendly and were all looking out for them-selves. They were rude and unkind."

"That's exactly the kind of people you're going to find in this city . . . you won't like it here," the wise man said.

Later in the day a different family was entering the city, and they stopped and asked the wise man the same question: "Can you tell us what kind of people we will find in this city?"

He responded as he did before, asking what the people were like in the city they'd come from. This family said, "Oh, the people in the city where we came from were friendly and kind people. They were so positive and encouraging."

"That's exactly the kind of people you will find in this city! You will love it here!" the wise man said with a smile.

*What we attract into our lives is not based on what we want but on what's inside of us.*

What that wise man was basing his conclusions on has been proven time and time again: what we attract into our lives is not based on what we want but on what's inside of us.

I remember as a boy getting in trouble and blaming it on the boys I was with. My mom didn't buy into my self-proclaimed innocence. In her mind I was guilty by way of association. She told me that "birds of a feather flock together." In time I realized there was a lot of truth in that statement.

If you put a hundred people in a room for a few hours, a magnetic-like current will begin to flow and like-minded people will be drawn toward each other. "Likes" will attract.

- Worrying people attract worrying people.
- Critical people attract critical people.
- Positive, upbeat people attract positive, upbeat people.
- People who are socially uncomfortable find one another on the perimeter of the room, out on the porch, or in the restrooms.
- Idea people attract idea people (and can't get enough of one another's ideas).

This phenomenon happens organically and naturally without orchestration or manipulation. People with the same interests and mind-sets are drawn together. This is why, regardless of what's going on around you, it's imperative that you persevere in your efforts to think favor-oriented thoughts.

Never forget: what's in you is more important than what's around you.

The thoughts in you impact and change the circumstances around you. If you put a messy person in a clean apartment, it won't be long until the apartment is messy. On the other hand, when you put a clean person in a messy apartment, it won't be long until the apartment is clean!

Favor-minded people impact the culture of the company they work for and the churches they attend. When a favor-minded person joins a team, he or she lifts the team's morale and makes the team better. When excellence is in a man or woman, it pulls excellence into that person's circumstances.

Never let circumstances determine what's in your mind. God's favor in you can and does dramatically change circumstances around you!

> *What's in you is more important than what's around you.*

The good news is that when our thoughts are confident and we approach life with expectation of the best, we experience the best possible outcome in every situation. When we approach that job interview with confidence that God is in control and he will give us the right words at the right time, we create a place for his favor to be *brought to us*. When we prepare to give that speech or take that test or do that audition and we envision ourselves doing well, we create a place for God's favor to be brought to us.

When we have positive expectations and confidence that God is for us, we experience the favor of God and man. We can't control the circumstances, but we can create the best possible outcome by being positive and favor minded in every situation.

You've probably heard the classic song "What a Wonderful World," first recorded by Louis Armstrong. The lyrics express wonder and gratitude concerning beautiful trees and flowers, the sky, a rainbow, babies crying, and people enjoying one another. The key phrase repeats several times, "And I think to myself, what a wonderful world."[2]

I've always loved that song—I even danced to it with my daughter during the father-daughter dance at her wedding. But I love it even more now after I noticed the line "I think to myself," because that's what I want to do! I want to think *that way* to myself.

A lot of people around you might wake up every day and their version is more like this:

I see traffic jams, cloudy skies, annoying people driving by, and I think to myself . . . what a difficult world.

Don't let what's around you get inside of you! Guard your mind because when you guard your mind, you put yourself in a position for God's best to come into your life. Always think something good to yourself.

There's a story, from when Jesus walked the earth, of a woman who had been hemorrhaging for twelve years. Jesus was near her hometown one day, and the Bible says, "She said to herself, 'If I only touch his cloak, I will be healed'" (Matthew 9:21).

Other people were saying negative things, but what she said to herself was more influencing on her than their comments. What she was verbalizing was affecting her physically—her body was moving in the direction of her internal dialogue. What if she had said, "I'll never get to him . . . it's not gonna change anything"? Her body would have slowed down, stopped, and she would have turned around.

> Always think something good to yourself.

Ultimately, what she said to herself became a self-fulfilling prophecy—she did make it to Jesus and she was healed.

Keep your mind full of the right thoughts and nothing will be able to stop blessings from coming to you.

Opportunity will knock on your door.

Promotion will come into your life.

Favor in your mind will draw favor into your life.

## THE SPACE BETWEEN THE TREES

The apostle Paul wrote in Philippians 4:8 that we should keep our minds on the right things. I call it the **"P4-8 principle,"** as a way of reminding myself to focus on the right things. Here's what it says:

> Whatever is true, whatever is noble, whatever is right, whatever
> is pure, whatever is lovely, whatever is admirable—if anything
> is excellent or praiseworthy—think about such things.

Sometimes what we focus on can even become the difference between life and death! Take skiing, for instance. Extreme downhill skiing is a wild sport. The skiers fly down slopes at kamikaze speeds, moving in and out of dangerous terrain. Oftentimes there are trees to get around and move past without slowing down.

One of the best extreme skiers ever is Kim Reichhelm. While doing an interview one day she was asked, "How do you keep from crashing?" She replied, "I look at the spaces between the trees."

What a brilliant idea to remember as we navigate the rough and rugged terrain of life! There are going to be immovable objects and unchangeable circumstances on your way to where you're going. But don't focus on what you can't change. Don't be distracted by what's in your way. Look at where you want to go, what you want to have, what you want to experience. Focus on the true, the noble, the right, and the excellent.

Keep your mind on the favor not the failure, the joy not the pain, and the prize not the price. As you go through life, stay focused on the spaces between the trees.

# Part 4

# When Good Things
# Take a Bad Turn

# What About "If"?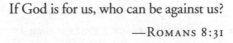

> If God is for us, who can be against us?
>
> —ROMANS 8:31

> If I were to say, "God, why me?" about
> the bad things, then I should have said,
> "God, why me?" about the good things
> that happened in my life.
>
> —ARTHUR ASHE

By this point in the book, I'm confident the "if" question may have slipped into the room, much like the proverbial pink elephant. I'm referring to the question that goes like this: "If God is so good, then why _____?"

That blank can be filled in with an almost infinite list of tragic, heartbreaking life events in our broken world.

Since this is a book about the goodness of God and his unending favor, am I presenting some kind of irreconcilable disconnect? How does the "if" question get answered? Is there an answer?

It is very important not to ignore this question because many people stumble and much faith is lost by the pain that fills that blank line in the "if" question after the word *why*.

Life throws us many curve balls, and Christ followers are not exempt! Jesus never promised a pain-free life. In fact, he said that we would face trouble in the world. But then he gives us the rest of the story and tells us to "be cheerful" and aware that he has overcome the world! (See John 16:33.)

When we experience hardship, we can easily lose sight of God's goodness. Hardship becomes the glare in our eyes, blocking our view and causing us to not see God's favor—even though it's always there.

Often people fill in the blank based on their own bad experiences. Let me be clear; there's no shame in wondering, *Why?* I don't think God gets upset when we wonder. Neither do I think that being a man or woman of faith means you have to have a lobotomy that removes your rational capability.

There are entire books written by some very intelligent writers who address the "why" question. I've read some of them and they are insightful and helpful, especially when you're in a season where you're wondering, *Why?* Having said that, however, my goal here is not to answer the "why" but to eliminate the "if," as in *If God is so good, then why* _____? Chances are the "why" will never be answered, but eliminating the "if" puts our feet on a stable, strong position. When we refuse to wonder if God is good, we find peace in times of pain.

We can confidently say and believe: God is good.

*But life is hard.*

A newlywed couple in our church has just had their second miscarriage. When they were single they were both on the "great catch" list: good looking, popular, full of life and energy. They both had great careers and were highly involved in church. There was a ton of energy and excitement around their wedding. They were the answer to each other's prayer, and God's goodness was at its all-time best for them. Favor felt good.

You could say that single life for them was like a Sunday filled with the emotional and spiritual highs of God's obvious favor. But if single life was like a Sunday, marriage brought a Monday experience into their lives. The wax had barely hardened on the candles from their wedding when married life presented them with the real-life disappointment and despair of Monday. Since they were not teenagers anymore when they got married, they were eager to start a family, excited to have children. It was natural for them to assume that the blessings they were enjoying were about to go to a whole new level as they began their lives together and started their family.

> *The greatest struggles in life are not the hardships themselves but the questions that the hardships create.*

The first time I saw them after their first miscarriage, the radiance that had always been on both of their faces was gone. It was easy to see that Monday was taking its toll on them. Their vibrant faces were now in survival mode. Their outgoing personalities were a bit more reserved. The confidence they had always shown had given way to uncertainty. As a pastor I knew that look in their eyes. They didn't have to say it. I knew their hearts were searching for the goodness of God in the midst of a real-life Monday challenge.

A pastor friend of mine, who is very successful in life and ministry, just sent me a private e-mail telling me that he has been diagnosed with cancer. Another friend, a beautiful mom of three, just found out that her husband has been having an affair. Still another friend and business leader just shared in confidence that he has no choice but to close down a business he has poured himself into and made successful in the prime years of his life. It's easy to see and talk about God's favor in the sunny, warm seasons of life but difficult to see when you face a cold, persistent rain.

Any kind of disappointment can distort your view of life and make you ask, "What happened to all those good things?" What I've discovered is that the greatest struggles in life are not the hardships themselves but the questions the hardships create.

## THEODICY

You may be familiar with the cliché "Life is hard; God is good." Maybe you've even said it to help get you through difficult times. If so, you're going to appreciate knowing that it's more than a cliché. It's a strong and solid theological truth. If you're like me you are going to be encouraged by the fact that some really smart people who were here before us have wrestled with questions such as, If God is good, then why is this happening? Why is injustice allowed, and why does life have to be so hard?

> *Life is hard;*
> *God is good.*

Philosophers and theologians refer to their conclusions on this topic with the complicated-sounding word *theodicy* (pronounced: thee od-euhsee), which is the name given to the study of how God's goodness exists *alongside* the pain, suffering, injustice, and inequality of life.

Our problem is that we tend to assume that if life is hard, then God must not be good. But it's not an either/or scenario—it's both!

*Life is hard; God is good.*

Here are five statements that pretty much summarize the deeper reasoning behind *Life is hard; God is good:*

- Although evil is an undeniable part of the world, the existence of evil cannot and never will cancel out the existence of good.
- Human beings don't have to offer explanations for why evil is allowed to exist, only that it does. And by the same rules of reason, good exists as well.

- In the same way that Adam through disobedience opened the door of undeserved hardship for all of us, Jesus through obedience opened the door of undeserved favor for all of us.
- The fact that we experience undeserved consequences for someone else's sin is now trumped by the fact that we experience undeserved favor for someone else's righteousness.
- God's undeserved goodness is not just equal to the undeserved hardship. It is surpassing in greatness.

The evidence of these two realities is front and center in our lives every day. But what's most important is which reality we choose to live our life from.

People who live from the "life is hard" reality see everything from that perspective. Sometimes when people are living from the "life is hard" reality they don't even want to hear good news. They have already decided that good news is not their reality. If you're talking about something positive or something good, they usually wait for a chance to quickly turn the conversation back to the "life is hard" reality. It has become such a way of life for them that they don't usually realize what they are doing.

The contrast between these two perspectives is so stark that it makes it difficult for people who choose to live in one or the other reality to get along. It's like oil and water—the two don't mix: You see things differently. You talk about things differently. You approach problems differently.

The presence of problems doesn't mean the absence of God. In the natural realm we know that the presence of clouds doesn't mean the absence of the sun. The clouds may temporarily block it, but the sun is still there. Even when you can't see the sun directly, you can see its light as evidence that it's there.

It is the same way with God's goodness and favor. There are times we may not be able to see those attributes directly, but that doesn't mean they're not there.

When we don't get the job we wanted or the person we were dating breaks up with us, we're often quick to assume God's favor is far away from us. But in time we come to realize that God was actually doing us a favor. He was saving us from hardship and struggle we would have had if we stayed in that relationship or got that job we thought we wanted.

We need to understand the true meaning of *hope*.

## ANCHORED IN HOPE

To be certain of God's goodness in the face of life's hardships is what the Bible refers to as being anchored in hope (see Hebrews 6:19).

It may come as a surprise, but the definition of the word *hope* in Scripture is the "expectation of good."[3] Let's not rush past that. Pause and think about it.

The reason I want to emphasize this is because the modern use of the word *hope* is typically thought of as "wishful thinking." Even though the definition includes the idea of expectation, for most people, having hope doesn't necessarily mean you're actually expecting something. For example, there's a totally different message being sent when a couple says, "We're hoping to have a baby" versus when they say, "We're expecting!" They don't even have to finish the sentence; everybody knows that a baby is on the way!

As followers of Christ we know all that is good comes from God. So we confidently experience hope as the *expectation of God's goodness*. Hope begins when we stop *wondering* and start *watching*. We are *expecting* to see the goodness of the Lord.

Being anchored in the goodness of God isn't always going to be a rational thing—a position you can explain, much less defend. It is just not reasonable that a person can be in the middle of a messy situation in life and be expecting God to do something good. But that's what being anchored in hope looks like. *Hope is a stubborn, unrelenting determination to not allow the hardships of life to downsize the bigness of God.* It's being in the middle of a storm and willing yourself to stay anchored in what you know about God's goodness for as long as it takes to ride out the rough weather.

On Christmas Eve in 1997, Karen Hartley, a thirty-three-year-old computer-software developer, wandered outside the Powder Mountain ski area in Utah and became lost in the wilderness. She was cold and alone on the mountain.

> *Hope begins when we stop wondering and start watching.*

The temperature was in the single digits. She knew that if she sat down, she would die. So she did more than just stay on her feet; she danced! She thought of the songs she could remember from the '90s and danced to those. Then she thought of songs from the '80s and danced to all of them. Then she thought of and danced to every song she could remember from the '70s. For eighteen hours she danced, knowing it was dance or die. Sometimes you have to dance where you are in order to get where you want to go. You have to sing and make music in your heart to keep yourself from drifting into negativity and discouragement. When God's goodness is not evident, you may need a song or a verse or a message to serve as the anchor.

Do whatever it takes and whatever you have to do to stay aware that your trials are just a temporary condition. You might have lost your bearings in a wilderness and not be sure how to get out, but *you can dance where you are.* You can dance with the expectation that your situation is changing for the better.

Your expectations are a creative force for bad or for good:

- If you expect life to be hard and unbearable, it will be. But if you expect to be strong and overcome adversity, you will.
- If you expect to feel weird when you get around people, you will not only feel weird—you'll act weird! But if you expect to be relaxed and confident in who you are, you will be.
- If you expect others to get all the good breaks and you not to get any, you won't. But if you expect to experience favor and see good things come your way, you will.

This doesn't mean that everything you expect to happen will happen. Neither does it mean that you won't be disappointed by things turning out differently than you expected. It does mean that the arc of your life will conform to your overall expectations.

I heard Charles Barkley, the former NBA star turned commentator, talking about his journey from growing up in a poor neighborhood to experiencing success that was beyond his wildest dreams. Statements like that can be confusing, because on one hand we're often told we have to have a dream before we can be successful. But then some successful people tell us that they never dreamed they would be as successful as they are! Sounds like a contradiction, right?

Here's the deal: having a dream, for most people, doesn't mean they know how it's all going to play out. But one thing all successful people have in common is that they had hope in something that was not yet evident in their lives.

Hope is where their commitment came from. And it's where the work ethic comes from—a deep internal expectation of good.

Charles Barkley worked hard on his game, put in the hours, stayed committed to the process, and remained in school at Auburn University because he had hope. His father had left early on, and his mother and grandmother raised him. He could have let his setbacks discourage him and cause him to quit, but hope kept him in the game. Eventually he saw good things happen because he expected good things to happen.

Yesterday's hope translates into fulfillment and satisfaction today. Scripture says, "Hope deferred makes the heart sick, but a longing fulfilled is a tree of life" (Proverbs 13:12). In other words, the sustaining substance of life is to identify and enjoy longings fulfilled on a daily basis. Your chance at another day is a longing fulfilled. Your wife or husband is a longing fulfilled. Your children are a longing fulfilled. Your house is a longing fulfilled.

Sometimes when I'm thinking too hard about stuff, I wake up tired before I get out of bed! The only way to make the day right is to engage in the expectation of something good, to go looking for it. The first good thing I look for is the hot, double-shot, nonfat latte that the Lord provides me every morning! (Okay, God and my wife or our barista.) I can't wait to have it in my hand! Just thinking about it and expecting to have it makes the world start to seem right!

The expectations that anchor your soul are not going to be the "some-day I will" bucket list. There may be great things to anticipate. But the hope that will anchor your soul is in looking forward to experiencing God's blessings every day in the simple things you enjoy doing, the people you enjoy seeing, the dinner you look forward to having, the gift you look forward to giving.

One thing that will happen when you start seeing life through the lens of God's favor is that the "if" becomes less important and can even go away. You start seeing the good in every situation! Your view of circumstances will start to cut through faulty world distortions and show you the good things that you overlooked before.

Favor starts to elbow its way back into the central frame of your perspective.

Blessings are now noticed.

The absoluteness of what you're seeing eliminates the "if" from the "*if* God is good . . ." question. When this happens you still may not answer the "why" question, but you'll feel less of a need to. When you eliminate the "if," God's goodness is no longer on trial. The evidence of blessings and favor becomes so obvious that a verdict is handed down. A decision is made. The conclusion is clear: *God is good!*

> *Our lives become better when we stop trying to answer the "why" and start eliminating the "if."*

In the Old Testament we find David in a season where he wasn't seeing good things due to life's distortions. But he set aside the down mood of the moment and relied on his history of good things. He had to eliminate the "if" and declare his certainty in times where he lacked clarity. He said it like this:

> I remain confident of this:
> I will see the goodness of the LORD. (Psalm 27:13)

Our lives become better when we stop trying to answer the "why" and start eliminating the "if." There's no justifiable reason for the "if." God's goodness is not obscure. It's not hidden. God's goodness is actually very evident. It's visible. It's tangible. It's real. Perhaps the greatest trait of all is that God's goodness is everlasting. It goes beyond our failures. It outlasts our fears. It remains with us in our sorrows.

## YOU CAN CHOOSE HOPE IN EVERY SITUATION AND CIRCUMSTANCE

We threw a big party when our one and only daughter, Jodi, got married. She's sort of a big deal to us, so when she found and fell in love with the best of the best, giving us the son we never had—it was cause for a huge celebration.

We were within days of the wedding when we got word that the doctors had told my mom, who lives in St. Louis, that she wouldn't be able to travel to Seattle for the big day. Being a close family, this was disappointing for all of us, especially my parents and Jodi.

They had purchased tickets. They had bought a new suit and dress for the occasion. But when the rest of the family and friends from the Midwest boarded planes, my parents had to stay behind.

Then somebody had an idea. Why not Webcast the wedding to their living room? Using our media cameras and equipment at church, we were able to set up a private link that would allow them to see the wedding at home over two thousand miles away. The wonder of technology!

A week or so after the wedding, I was visiting my mom and dad in St. Louis when a family friend slipped up to me privately and asked if anyone had told me "how the wedding had played out in St. Louis"?

I said I had heard it went well and there had been no complications with the Webcast.

She said, "No, I mean did anyone tell you about your mom and dad?"

I was confused about what she meant, and so she continued to share with me that on the afternoon of the wedding, she'd received a call from my dad asking her to pick up some flowers and a corsage for my mom and to order some food to be brought to the house. She had picked up the flowers and food and delivered them to their home and was visiting with the technician who was handling the Webcast. She then told me how moments before the wedding was to begin, my folks came out of the bedroom, and much to her surprise, my dad was dressed up in his suit and my mom in her dress that they had bought for the wedding. My dad carefully pinned the corsage on my mom and then pulled his chair up next to hers in front of the television screen and celebrated our big day with us!

When things don't go as you want in life, you don't have to sulk in self-pity. You don't have to feel sorry for yourself, and you don't have to drift into wondering and questioning God. You can eliminate the "if" and anchor yourself in the facts and reasoning that *God's goodness is surpassing in greatness to life's hardships.*[4]

# Chapters 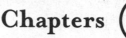 13

And we know that in all things God
works for the good of those who love
him, who have been called according
to his purpose.

—ROMANS 8:28

If you're going through hell, keep going.

—WINSTON CHURCHILL

Just as a good book is made up of many chapters, so a good life has many chapters. And each of life's chapters fits into a larger story and provides context, detail, and depth.

This understanding does not alleviate the pain in life, but it does help us stay steady as we walk through the inevitable valleys of life on a fallen planet.

All of the times when things are good or bad—or not all that memorable—chapters of a larger story are written.

No two chapters are completely alike, and they are not supposed to be. Chapters are chapters—not the whole story. They are *not meant* to be the story but are like ingredients in a recipe, included to contribute to the flavor of something much better and greater.

Some people make the mistake of turning a chapter of their life into the story of their life. They say things like "That's the story of my life . . .

a day late and a dollar short." Or "Two steps forward and three back." Or "If anything bad is gonna happen, it's gonna happen to me!"

What they don't realize is that the "day late" or the "dollar short" was supposed to be a chapter. When people make a chapter their story, they sabotage the bigger, greater story of their life.

The good news is that God is doing something good in every chapter:

> And we know that in all things God works for the good of those
> who love him, who have been called according to his purpose.
> (Romans 8:28)

First, notice it doesn't say "in all good things God works." It says *in all things* God works—the good, the bad, the ugly, the pain, the mess-ups. *God works.*

Second, notice that God doesn't just work to get us through it. He works in all things *for the good!* No matter what the chapter is like, it's all part of a bigger story and it's all good. Which is how you want to frame struggles and disappointments in your life. Frame them in the "It's all good" frame, or at least in the "It will be good" frame.

In 2004 Sheila and I had an accident on a motorbike on the island of Bermuda. It definitely wasn't a good thing. I broke my pelvis and lay on a two-lane highway, fortunate that the vehicles didn't hit me, because I couldn't get up to move off the road. Those were horrific moments. (Thankfully, Sheila had only bumps and bruises.)

It just so happened (if you believe that things like this "just happen") that a group of off-duty Bermuda police officers were jogging at the exact spot where I went down. Within moments they had traffic stopped in both directions and had called for an ambulance. My daughter, Jodi, who was riding her own motorbike behind Sheila and me, now had my head in her lap, and I could hear her praying. As I looked upward I saw a strong masculine black arm extended over my daughter's head, palm down toward me, and heard a booming voice say, "Father, I come into agreement with this prayer today."

> *If I could have a do-over, I would fight to keep that painful event as a chapter in my life.*

*What?*

Not only were the police there at just the right moment, but a praying policeman? That was the first big sign that in my "all things," God was there! Because of the speed with which they got me to the hospital my life was saved. The pelvis houses a main blood supply, so when it's broken there can be severe internal bleeding, which some people do not survive.

Later, after returning home and getting a few weeks of healing under my belt, one of our friends and team members asked me, "If you could reverse time and take this incident out of your life, would you do it?"

When I took just a second to consider it, I remembered the people I had met, the things I had witnessed, and the incredible works God had done. There was no question in my mind: if I could have a do-over, I would *fight* to keep that painful, difficult, frustrating event as a chapter in my life.

## SOME OF THE WORST CHAPTERS MAKE THE BEST STORIES

Think about your favorite books or stories: the greater the adventure, adversity, and challenges, the greater the story. This is often illustrated by the lives of well-known people. What if you didn't know anything about them other than their worst chapter? Here are some examples:

- Tyler Perry is a famous actor, producer, and screenwriter. If you were to grab a chapter from Perry's story, you would read about a young boy born in extreme poverty who had an abusive father. Another chapter would tell you about a twenty-eight-year-old man who was living in his car, homeless.
- Bill Gates is currently the richest person in the world. If you were to read a chapter of his story, you would encounter a young guy whose first company, called Traf-O-Data, failed miserably.
- Bethany Hamilton won first place in the Explorer Women's division of the National Scholastic Surfing Association National Championships. If you were to read only a few pages out of her story, you would find a girl who at age thirteen was attacked by a shark and lost her left arm.
- Oprah Winfrey is the famous all-time queen of television talk shows. In one chapter of her story you would read about a young girl who was repeatedly molested by a cousin, an uncle, and a family friend, then ran away from home and, at age fourteen, gave birth to a baby boy who died shortly after birth.
- Franklin Roosevelt was one of America's most respected and memorable presidents. In one chapter of his life, after vacationing in Canada, he developed polio, which eventually left him paralyzed from the waist down.
- Steven Spielberg is one of the most prolific filmmakers of all time and currently a trustee of the University of Southern California. If you read only one chapter of his story, you would read about a young man who was rejected by the USC School of Cinematic Arts—twice.[5]

Isn't it interesting that buried in the stories of successful people are chapters that don't reveal the whole story but were important parts in the overall story? And don't the worst chapters of a good story make the whole story even better?

*God never writes us off because of bad chapters.*

This is why we can't ever let the loss of a job, business, or house make us believe that's the whole story of our lives! This is why we can't allow a physical condition, an unplanned pregnancy, a divorce, or memories of sexual abuse to cause us to label our lives as failures.

God never writes us off because of bad chapters. He is always ready to stand by us, heal us, and restore us if we are willing and determined to move on to new life chapters. The great thing about God is that he even specializes in taking the worst chapters and using them to make our story even better.

## YOU DON'T DECIDE THE CHAPTERS, BUT HOW YOU FRAME THEM DECIDES THE STORY

At our house we recorded and watched the television drama series *24*. If you're familiar with it, you know that every episode ended with a cliff-hanger. The suspense was through the ceiling as we wondered what our main man, Jack Bauer, was going to do! We all know that the fictional star of the show didn't get to decide the chapters, but his response would decide the story. So we followed along with him wondering, *What's Jack going to do now?*

Your life is the same way. *You're not the only character in your story.*

- You don't decide what family you're born into.
- You don't decide what neighborhood you grow up in or which school you attend.
- You don't get to pick your siblings.

- You usually don't get to pick your classmates or your teachers.
- You don't control what others do and say.
- You don't control the economy.
- You don't write the plots in your story.
- You don't pick which problems you'll have.
- You don't know which friends will turn on you.
- You don't decide what accidents you will be involved in.
- You don't choose what sickness or infections you will deal with.
- You don't strategize to be rejected.
- You don't plan to be abandoned.

But make no mistake about it—it's still your story!

And only you can decide how you frame the chapters, which decides the story.

Between the plot being formed and your response to it, you have a chance to frame every situation into a perspective. You get an opportunity to decide how you're going to see it. What some see as the end, others see as a chance to begin again. When some see the loss, others see the gain. When some see what they can't do, others see what they can do. When some see the problems, others see the possibilities. What some see as a reason to be bitter, others see as an opportunity to be better.

## FRESH FAVOR

The manna God provided for Israel in the wilderness was a huge demonstration of fresh favor.

It started like this: The Israelites were running short on food, only to wake up one morning and see the ground covered with manna. Chaos broke out as everyone scrambled to pick up all that they could gather in their pockets, baskets, and other containers. Their thinking was, *We better get all we can while we can.* In their minds, that kind of heavenly provision would be short lived, so they decided to ration the gathered supply and make it last as long as possible.

What seemed like a reasonable plan was spoiled, however, when that night while they were sleeping, maggots infested their stored manna. God sent them a message that said, *"Yesterday's favor is not today's favor."* He clearly did not want them to eat today's leftovers tomorrow. Rather than trying to preserve today's favor, he wanted them to engage every day with an expectation of *fresh* favor. God wanted them to believe that there's always more where that came from—more blessing, more provision, more of God's favor (see Exodus 16).

Another thing that happened was that after the Israelites ate the manna, they complained that it was not "the same" as the corn and melons they had enjoyed while in Egypt. The form of favor had changed, and they were sentimentally attached to the old form of favor, which hindered them from fully appreciating the new season of favor (see Numbers 11).

> God's favor was on yesterday, yesterday—it's not on yesterday, today!

Here's the takeaway: As good as yesterday may have been in your life, God doesn't want you living there. He has new experiences, new discoveries, and new opportunities for you in the current season of your life.

The best way to honor the past is to not get stuck in it! Stay creative and confident in today's supply of fresh favor. One of the biggest mistakes we can make is to get sentimentally attached to a past season of God's favor versus moving forward to experience a new season of his favor.

God's favor was on yesterday, yesterday—it's not on yesterday, today!

The psalmist said, "This is the day the LORD has made; we will rejoice and be glad in it" (Psalm 118:24, NKJV). He didn't say he will rejoice in yesterday; he said he will rejoice in today!

God's favor is new every day!

Live in today!

Expect great things today!

Draw on God's favor for today!

The reality is that you may have hit the "I'm tired" button because you are emotionally depleted. Or maybe you are tempted to tap out because you think you're getting too old to still make a difference.

When you feel weary it may mean it's time for some course correction or new habits. You might want to get some outside voices speaking wisdom and clarity into your foggy set of circumstances. But the main thing I want to impress on you is that God plans that the second half of your life will be the best half of your life!

God's favor isn't finished when you feel tired or weary. God has fresh favor waiting for you just on the other side of this season you're in. He will refresh you, renew your strength, and make you strong *all the days* of your life!

You may still be young, but you're not too young to start thinking about staying strong and finishing strong!

I love the words of Caleb who, when he was eighty-five years old, said, "I'm still as strong today as I was in my youth. . . . Now give me this mountain" (see Joshua 14:11–12).

When Abraham was ninety-nine years old, God appeared to him and said, "I will make you into a great nation, and I will bless you; I will make your name great, and you will be a blessing" (Genesis 12:2).

Cam Townsend, founder of Wycliffe Bible Translators, flew to Moscow and began learning Russian to assist in Bible translation work in the

Caucasus. The nation was still under the iron grip of communism, and he was seventy-two years young.

Colonel Harland Sanders was sixty-five years old when he started actively franchising his chicken recipe. His face later became the second most recognized in America.

John Wesley preached over 40,000 sermons and traveled 225,000 miles (his horse had never heard of kilometers). But get this: these figures belong only to the latter part of his life, from age thirty-six to eighty-eight.

President Ronald Reagan was seventy-six years old when he pointed to the Berlin Wall and said those famous words that ushered in a new era: "Mr. Gorbachev, tear down this wall!"

No matter your age or circumstances, your past supply is not your last supply! There is no end to the favor of God. It has no quota and no limits. The Lord's eyes are on you for your entire lifetime! Not a day goes by that he's not watching over you: "The LORD will watch over your coming and going both now and forevermore" (Psalm 121:8).

He has fresh, new ways to provide for you and bless others through you in every chapter of your life.

# Favor Forward (14)

Is there anyone still left of the house of
Saul to whom I can show kindness for
Jonathan's sake?

—KING DAVID, 2 SAMUEL 9:1

You cannot do a kindness too soon, for
you never know how soon it will be too
late.

—RALPH WALDO EMERSON

D o you think Bill Gates of Microsoft needs anything?
That seems like a ridiculous question maybe, and I don't know
Gates or what he might be short on. But I know myself and have known
many people, and I conclude that every person alive needs as much love,
encouragement, respect, and purpose as everyone else. And Gates, even
with all his riches, wishes to have his basic needs met in the same way the
rest of us do—through life-giving supportive relationships with others.

Where I'm going with this is that one of the best ways to find relief
from our own pain and inadequate answers to the "why me, why this?"
questions of life is to find others we can help to overcome their pain and
challenges. This is the pattern God has given us, demonstrated most
completely and perfectly by Jesus, who gave himself for others—and asks
us to do the same.

## DAVID'S QUESTION

There's an illustration of this kind of above-and-beyond caring for others in the life of the great King David.

The thoughts of David, once only a lowly shepherd boy, were swimming in pools of remembrance. The story seemed almost too good to be true—where *he was now* compared to where he was then—staggering! Somehow a dynasty reserved only for those in the bloodline of royalty had opened up to include him. He knew the events that had led up to his becoming the king of Judah, but he was still incredibly fascinated by how it had all happened.

Obviously, God's favor was on his life.

Perhaps that's what he was thinking about on this day when waves of gratitude overwhelmed him and he suddenly blurted out a question, which caused all those around him to scurry in search of an answer. It was an unexpected, spontaneous question prompted in a moment of reflection, and no one in his immediate airspace knew the answer. So they went looking for someone who did, and it wasn't long until a man named Ziba came to stand before the king. David asked him the same question: "**Is there anyone still left of the house of Saul to whom I can show kindness for Jonathan's sake?**" (2 Samuel 9:1).

> *The greatest expression of gratitude we have is to pay it forward.*

We've all experienced some unsolicited kindness, when for some reason people wanted to show us kindness, to grace us with their favor—perhaps parents, mentors, teachers, coaches, relatives, neighbors, pastors, and friends who played significant roles in helping us get to where we are today. They showed us favor we had not earned, and maybe now because we've lost touch with them, it's impossible to thank them personally. Or maybe it's just hard emotionally to express accurately the gratitude we feel.

So the greatest expression of gratitude we may have available to us now is to pay it forward—to pass on kindness to another person.

This is exactly the state of mind David was in as he remembered his friend Jonathan, the son of the previous king, Saul. Jonathan had been the heir apparent to the throne David now occupied. Their relationship had been cemented by an agreement to preserve and protect each other no matter what. This is what David was recalling that day when he asked his question. He was on a mission that no one in the palace could fully understand or comprehend.

I love the simplicity of David's question. He did not ask, "Is there anyone who is deserving? Is there anyone who could help me in the business of the kingdom? Is there anyone with skills? Is there anyone who is qualified to lead our military?" No, he simply asked, "Is there anyone? Just *anyone* of the house of Saul?"

Ziba, the servant who had been summoned, knew about only one son of Jonathan—a young man who had suffered a severe fall that left him crippled for life. Ziba said, "There is still a son of Jonathan; he is lame in both feet" (2 Samuel 9:3).

Why did Ziba add the information about the injured feet? Maybe he thought this deformity would eliminate that son as a candidate for the king's kindness. Perhaps he thought the king would be embarrassed in some way by having a crippled man in his presence.

But the words were hardly out of Ziba's mouth when King David quickly asked another question: "Where is he?"

"He is at the house of Makir son of Ammiel in Lo Debar," Ziba answered (verse 4).

Lo Debar was a desolate place, known for its extreme poverty and barely survivable conditions. Now all the personal, unpleasant, and unappealing information that Ziba knew was out on the table. This son of Jonathan was definitely not the kind of person one would expect a king to be interested in. But David never showed an ounce of hesitation.

> So King David had him brought from Lo Debar, from the house of Makir son of Ammiel.
>
> When Mephibosheth son of Jonathan, the son of Saul, came to David, he bowed down to pay him honor.
>
> David said, "Mephibosheth!"
>
> "At your service," he replied.
>
> "Don't be afraid," David said to him, "for I will surely show you kindness for the sake of your father Jonathan. I will restore to you all the land that belonged to your grandfather Saul, and you will always eat at my table." (verses 5–7)

The difference a day can make! The marginalized, disenfranchised, socially excluded Mephibosheth had been lifted out of Lo Debar by the extravagant kindness of the king. Typically, when we consider kindness, we think of offering greetings and smiles, opening doors, buying someone coffee. But when David said he wanted to show someone kindness, he was thinking way outside our normal box. To David kindness meant much more than a small act. To him it was a complete game-changing, life-altering demonstration of favor that would impact the recipient's life continually from that day forward.

• • •

This story, in and of itself, not only provokes great sentiment, but my hope is that you see the uncanny analogies between this story and our own. Our story is the story of fallen humanity. We were born as part of God's family but were crippled by sin—marginalized, disenfranchised, and excluded. Because of a covenant our Father made on our behalf, we have received unconditional, unmerited, unsolicited, and unending favor.

Our story is not just one of mercy. Our story is a story of God's extravagant favor. We are not mere recipients of compassion. We are not placed on a subsidy food program so we can survive in Lo Debar. Because of God's extravagant favor, we are invited to experience life in his presence in spite of our flawed condition. God decided that nothing about us disqualifies us. We are summoned to his house and welcomed to his table.

> Our story is a story of God's extravagant favor.

My point is that when we, like David, recognize the great favor that's been shown to us, there's only one natural response: We want to show favor to others. We have the opportunity to share the same experience with others—to "pay forward" the favor shown to us by Jesus. It's his favor that has been transferred to us, making us the recipients of unearned, undeserved, and unmerited favor.

## GRATITUDE SAYS, "DO SOMETHING"

So back to Bill Gates. I was in a restaurant in the Seattle area and noticed Gates and his wife, Melinda, sitting in a corner booth. Seeing him brought to mind the tremendous generosity that they have demonstrated over the years in our city and around the world. As I sat there I included myself, our church family, and so many others as beneficiaries of all the jobs they've created and the generosity he and Melinda have shown through their foundation.

After getting the waiter's attention I told him I would like to buy their meal. You would have thought I had slapped him. He looked at me with disbelief and asked me what I meant. So I repeated myself and requested that he bring me their check. He said he needed to speak with his manager. The next thing I knew they had asked Gates if it was okay and pointed me out to him as "the guy who wants to buy your meal." I expected it to be quiet and anonymous, rather than raising suspicions of ulterior motives.

The waiter returned and said it was okay but wanted to clarify that I had no expectations of any kind of reciprocation—that I genuinely just wanted to buy their dinner.

I understand the waiter's and manager's concerns, but what they didn't realize is that I was acting from a place of gratitude, as one who has been a recipient of blessing and favor, and was simply wanting to do a small favor for someone else. Again, Bill Gates didn't need anything from me. It wasn't about him receiving a favor; it was about me passing *favor forward*.

# Part 5

# A Life of Good Things

# Favor Dynamics

> Jesus grew in wisdom and stature, and
> in favor with God and man.
>
> —Luke 2:52

> O Lord, please hear my prayer! . . .
> Please help me now as I go in and ask
> the king for a great favor—put it into
> his heart to be kind to me.
>
> —Nehemiah 1:11 (TLB)

Most of the time, God's favor does not fall from the sky like the manna did for the Israelites during their extended camping trip. As with so much of life, favor is bound up in relationships. So allow me to offer seven key insights on what I'll call favor dynamics.

## 1. Favor flows to people through people

I've never received the resources we needed in our ministry in an envelope with God as the sender and a return address of heaven. But I've been absolutely amazed as I witnessed God provide for us through people who were compelled or moved by God to give.

One example of that was when the economic collapse of 2007–08 hit the Northwest, and many of the business leaders in our church were unable to give as they had previously. It was at that time that some folks I had never met and who did not attend our church (or any church) sent a generous check to our ministry. Our TV program had caught their eye, and they had felt inspired to give.

In the months following they sent checks to our church and TV ministry in various amounts totaling over $200,000. Our TV program is good, but I can assure you it wasn't the lighting, special effects, or glamour of the television program that caught the eye of the viewer during that season!

This is one example of the way God releases his favor. There's absolutely no explanation for the crucial timing or the over-the-top generous giving that occurred other than God's favor flowing *to people through people.*

Stories in the Bible reveal how God's people were constantly "catching the eye" of someone in a position of power who was capable of blessing them:

- *Joseph caught the eye of the king of Egypt's cupbearer,* who brought his name up to the king, beginning the process of Joseph's journey from prison to the palace, from nameless to famous.
- *Ruth caught the eye of Boaz,* who inquired about her gleaning in his field and ended up making her his wife. Ruth went from gleaning in the field to owning it!
- *David caught the eye of Samuel,* who anointed him king and opened the door for David the shepherd to become David the king.
- *Esther caught the eye of everyone* and especially the king, who heard and granted her request that saved her people from genocide.

I could add many more names to this list of favor flowing to people through people. So, why would it be any different for you? It's not! Right now God has people in your life that are the expression of his favor toward you. They are there because he wants to use them to bless you, encourage you, and even open doors for you. They are not in your life by accident or coincidence. They are there as part of God's plan of favor in your life. Your responsibility is to recognize them and treat them with honor.

> *Right now God has people in your life that are the expression of his favor toward you.*

When Sheila and I came to the Northwest from the Midwest, we took over a small church that was out of money and unable to make its mortgage payments. So with minimal resources, Sheila and I moved into a small apartment and certainly did not have the funds to have our furniture moved.

One day, as I was talking to the banker overseeing our church business, he asked if we were all moved in. After talking a few minutes, he offered to contact a friend who had a trucking company. One thing led to another, and within a few days our furniture was on a truck coming from St. Louis to Seattle. The trucking company charged us a minimal delivery fee because they had some other deliveries in our area.

Now for the rest of the story. Almost twenty-five years after we made this move, my mom passed away. And a couple of years after that my father met a fantastic lady and remarried.

After all those years, I had a chance to meet the owner of the company who had moved our furniture for us. Of course I knew the name of the trucking company and had been aware that the owners were Christians—and that they had felt compelled to do something to help a twenty-six-year-old preacher and his wife who couldn't afford to pay for a move. What I couldn't have imagined was that the woman my dad would marry decades later was the *owner* of that trucking company!

Those trucking company owners had no obligation to us—we had never met. The same was true for the banker who made it all happen. I didn't even ask anyone for help. These folks just had a desire to do something to help someone else.

### 2. Honor up, honor down, honor all around

How we bestow honor on others is such a powerful key to the favor God has for our lives! It's important to honor not only the people above you but also the people beneath you and around you. So often we want to rush past the "unimportant people" to get to those we think might be able to open doors of favor for us. It's easy to be so enamored by successful people that we see them as the ones we have to cultivate relationships with in order to be successful ourselves. You might even be thinking now of what you can do to catch their eye!

But that's not how favor works. First of all, God is working his favor not just through the "special people." No, oftentimes God's favor comes through the people who are not the supertalented or most successful people around us. It's not always the person above you that God's supply of favor comes through. Sometimes it's the people around you or even beneath you who usher God's favor into your life.

> *Often God's favor comes through the people we least expect it from.*

The door opener for Joseph was a fellow inmate when he was in prison.

King Saul was so jealous of David that he despised him and did everything in his power to oppose him. So God used Saul's son Jonathan as an expression of his favor in David's life. Jonathan loved David and had a key role in David becoming king.

David also experienced a groundswell of favor from the men who surrounded him in his pre-king days. The favor he had with them as their leader was off the charts in loyalty and support.

In fact I've often wondered what kind of leader it is that men will risk their lives to get him a drink of water from his hometown well. David's "mighty men" heard him say around a battlefield campfire that he wished he had a drink from the well of Bethlehem. David didn't ask or suggest that they go get it. He just said what we all say when we think of a favorite drink or food—"I'd love to have a nice hot cocoa latte right now!" We may mean it, but we're just imagining it.

Yet that night three men risked their lives by slipping through enemy lines to bring David the water he longed for from the well of Bethlehem (see 2 Samuel 23:13–17). That's huge favor!

Don't limit God's supply of favor to you by thinking it will come only through a select few rich and famous people. Often his favor comes through the people we least expect it from, which is all the more reason for us to treat everyone—above, beneath, and around us—with dignity and honor.

The other thing that's important to realize is that you don't have to figure out how to catch the eye of the people who usher God's favor into your life. Just be mindful of all people around you. Treat people like you want to be treated. Be kind. Be considerate. Be helpful. Be willing to go the extra mile without strings attached. Isn't that what true honor is all about, anyway? You'll be surprised at how having a good attitude toward others will bring you into places of favor.

### 3. Relax—God knows what you need

Confidence in God's favor releases us from the urge to manipulate or orchestrate favor from people.

There's an old saying, "It's not what you know; it's who you know." I don't think anyone would argue with the fact that knowing and being connected with the right people is advantageous in life. But just like God didn't need King Saul's cooperation to promote David, God's favor for your future doesn't rest in the hands of another person. The doorkeepers in your professional life won't always see you coming or recognize your talent and ability. The power brokers won't always identify you as the person they are looking for. But that's okay. God's plan doesn't rest in the perfect intuition or flawless analysis of those influential people in your life.

Through Isaiah's writings God said:

I summon a bird of prey;
    from a far-off land, a man to fulfill my purpose.
What I have said, that I will bring about;
    what I have planned, that I will do. (Isaiah 46:11)

In this scripture God is letting us know that he can bring favor in our lives even if he has to reach outside the circle of people whom we might think he needs to use.

A few years back I was looking for a personal assistant. With the help of an outside consultant, we had a description on paper of the exact type of person I needed, but we couldn't seem to find that person anywhere. One day as I expressed my frustration to our consultant, he said to me that he felt the person we were looking for was right under our noses. This consultant was not only a corporate coach but also a great man of God to whom I had seen God reveal things before, but that day I was struggling with what he said. We had tried really hard to recruit someone.

Then he said with greater urgency, "Pastor, I know we've looked through the files of all your employees before, but I feel like we're supposed to look again. Would you please have the files brought up to your office? And while I'm still on the phone with you, I want us to look for this person again."

So, a bit reluctantly, I called for a member of the administrative team to bring all the files to my office. Then, with my advisor on speakerphone directing her, she started giving him test results of different staff members. When she read the test results of one person who was at that time the receptionist, he said, "That's your person! That's the one you're looking for!"

It took some convincing before I saw it. But that person, Toni, is my current personal assistant and has proven to be the perfect person for that position. I now know (and I'm quite sure Toni knows too) that without a doubt God brought her from North Carolina to our city, then to our church, next to our reception desk, and finally to the key role she has played in our lives for almost twenty years. Believe me when I tell you she's as good as they come and has been an incredible blessing to us—another example of God's favor!

Hopefully as you're reading this, your confidence in God's favor is growing stronger. That confidence frees us from needing to obligate, push, manipulate, or beg people to do something for us. We can allow God to do his thing and go to work on our behalf.

### 4. Somebody else's favor is not your favor

Do yourself a favor—don't compare somebody else's favor with your favor! God has favor with your name on it, tailored just for you!

My daughter, Jodi, and her cousin, Kent, both loved their grandma's red velvet cake. When Grandma would make a cake, they would pounce on it the minute it had icing. As they got older they started hiding a slice from each other so they could have the last piece themselves. One time, months after they both went home, their grandma found a dried-up piece of cake that had been hidden by one of them and apparently forgotten.

If your idea of favor is that it is like a cake with only so many slices, you will end up competing with others for as much of the favor cake as you can get! Then, as other people experience favor, you will think their favor automatically leaves less for you. You will be tempted to compare and compete with them for favor. But when you know that God has a unique, specific favor planned for you, you will not only celebrate other people's favor but be confident in God's favor for you.

One of the ways we can limit God's favor is in assuming that people we admire or look up to have taken all the "favor parking spots," and we are left to drive around looking for one to open up. But in God's "favor lot," no matter how many have found a spot, there's one where no one else can park; it's saved for only you.

God hasn't left you out, and he didn't run out of favor before you came along. Be confident and secure in knowing that God has favor reserved with your name on it.

### 5. Seek the success of others

One of the common ways people sabotage their own success is when they unconsciously start competing with the people they were meant to collaborate with. One way this can happen is that rather than coming alongside a leader God put them next to, they start competing with that leader. This can be their manager at work or it might be their team leader at church. It can be a friend or partner in business.

Proverbs says, "The one who guards a fig tree will eat its fruit, and whoever protects their master will be honored" (27:18). All of us must recognize and care for the fig trees in our lives, which after our spouse, children, and friends might be a customer, project, company, employer, pastor, team, assistant, or client. We reap the benefits when we look after those who produce a harvest of good things for us.

You increase your own chance of experiencing favor when your goal is lifting up the people around you. If that happens best by being the leader, then lead. But if that happens best by coming alongside and supporting another leader, then follow.

Bob Richards is the only man to win two Olympic gold medals in the pole vault. When he was trying to break the record held by Dutch Warmerdam, he kept falling short. After trying everything from various coaches to different vaulting methods, he finally called Dutch and asked if he would help him. Something in Dutch couldn't say no. He agreed to become Bob's coach and added eight inches to Bob's best vault. Dutch helped Bob break Dutch's own Olympic record.

> God will use the greatness in other people to bring out the greatness in us.

Bob could have been too competitive with Dutch and too prideful to let himself learn from Dutch. But instead Bob honored Dutch, and Dutch also humbly helped Bob break the record. When Bob honored the gift and talent that Dutch had, his own life went to another level. When Dutch unselfishly helped Bob, he became part of a new world record!

In much the same way, God will use the greatness in other people to bring out the greatness in us: "As iron sharpens iron, so one person sharpens another" (Proverbs 27:17).

## 6. People who oppose you can't stop God's favor

I have some news for you: there will always be people who don't like you.

But you're not alone. Being a Christ follower means that some people won't want to be around you. You may not be the first person on the call list when some of your friends at work or school are looking to go out and party.

I urge you, though, not to embrace the martyr mind-set too quickly. There's another side of the coin for you, and that is the unexplainable, unsolicited favor that other people will be compelled to show you.

For twenty-one years a man named Laban cheated his employee Jacob out of his wages. Laban lied to, mistreated, and took advantage of

Jacob. Maybe there were days when Jacob felt discouraged, but he some-how remained poised and confident. Jacob kept his cool, staying in char-acter and standing tall in every setback and every injustice. If you had come along in the fifth year or the twelfth year and compared Jacob to Laban, you might have been tempted to associate the favor on Laban's life with his unethical, ruthless, and inconsiderate approach to business. You also might have thought, *Poor Jacob, he works so hard . . . he's so honest . . . and he never gets ahead.* You may have also been tempted to assume that Laban's shrewd and unethical approach to business was the way to get ahead. But those conclusions would be like judging a meal that's not yet cooked. The truth is that Laban was doing well because God was using Jacob to bless Laban's busi-ness. Nobody, especially Laban, saw it coming. But eventually all of his business got turned over to Jacob! (See Genesis 31.)

> *Nothing and no one can stop God's favor in your life!*

However, it may take time to see God's favor.

After over twenty years, Jacob walked away with Laban's daughters, grandkids, livestock, and more wealth than Laban could ever have dreamed of having. *People can't stop God's favor!* The Bible says, "Good people obtain favor from the LORD, but he condemns those who devise wicked schemes" (Proverbs 12:2).

You may feel overlooked or that you've been denied opportunities. Maybe you feel that people have been biased against you, misjudged you, or even held you back from something you deserved. Here's what I want to remind you: if you keep your poise and stay in character, nothing and no one can stop God's favor in your life! It may take some time before you see it, but God can use even the Labans of your life to bless you.

"Then you will win favor and a good name in the sight of God and man" (Proverbs 3:4).

### 7. Stay connected to your God-assigned connections

You don't have to chase after anyone, because God will assign people to you. When he does, your success is connected to those people. You can experience what I call a *favor splash* from them to you.

A favor splash is favor experienced by being with the right people, in the right place, at the right time. It could be the person you work for. It could be the pastor you serve. It could be a teacher, mentor, or coach. The point is to never underestimate how their presence in your life is impacting your ongoing success.

It's easy to take these people for granted. Familiarity causes us to underestimate the benefit of having them in our lives. Nehemiah was just a cupbearer in a foreign land, but the connection he had with the king opened doors and positioned him in a place of tremendous influence. Nehemiah honored the king, even from a distance, and he acted within the parameters given to him. Nehemiah represented the king and at the same time fulfilled the desires God had put in his heart.

I don't know to whom you might be assigned, but there will always be personality differences and opportunities for conflict and offense. If you can keep from being irritated by your differences or intimidated by them—and if you can resist the temptation to compete or compare yourself with those people, to keep your heart free from jealousy and envy—God will use those people to bless, advance, and increase you.

# Favor Shifts

The angel of God that had been leading
the camp of Israel now **shifted** and got
behind them. And the Pillar of Cloud that
had been in front also **shifted** to the rear.

—Exodus 14:19, The Message,
emphasis added

Two roads diverged in a wood, and I—
I took the one less traveled by,
And that has made all the difference.

—Robert Frost

Launch out into the deep." That's what Jesus said to Simon, the proprietor of a fishing business at the Sea of Galilee (Luke 5:4, KJV). Simon had fished all night and caught nothing. Then, as he was cleaning his boat and nets, Jesus—who had been sitting in a boat nearby—turned to him and encouraged him to try something different.

Let's pick up the story in Luke where we're told that Simon was resistant to this whole idea of putting the boat back in the water. He'd heard about Jesus but wasn't a follower.

Simon answered,

"Master, we've worked hard all night and haven't caught anything. But because you say so, I will let down the nets."

When they had done so, they caught such a large number of
fish that their nets began to break. So they signaled their partners
in the other boat to come and help them, and they came and
filled both boats so full that they began to sink. (verses 5–7)

So these tired, weary fishermen, who had fished all night and caught
nothing, went from empty boats one hour to full boats the next hour.
Right when they thought it was quitting time, they had an opportunity
to do something out of the ordinary, and when they did, God caused a
divine shift in their lives. Rather than going home with nothing, those
fishermen headed to the market with two boatloads of fish!

Not only that, but Simon also went on to become Simon Peter, one
of Jesus's disciples and the voice of the church in the New Testament!

When God asks us to do something out of the ordinary, it is because
he wants to do something out of the ordinary for us. A slight shift in our
attitudes, routines, perspective, hearts, and choices can be the "internal
shift" that positions us to experience a "holy shift" in our lives.

Big things happened that day on the Sea
of Galilee because of Peter's midsentence internal shift: "But because you say so, I will let
down the nets."

What internal shift in you might trigger
an avalanche of new blessings? Are you just
one internal shift away from experiencing an
increase of favor with God and man? A shift

> When God asks us
> to do something out
> of the ordinary, he
> wants to do some-
> thing out of the
> ordinary for us.

may not be about doing something different but about doing the same
thing in a different way.

There was another time in Scripture just after Jesus's resurrection
when the disciples had fished all night and caught nothing. Jesus told
them to fish on the opposite side of the boat, and when they did, their

catch of fish was so large they were unable to haul the net in. Sometimes we do things in a way that we've always done them, but we're not getting the results we used to get. That doesn't necessarily mean we're supposed to do something different, but maybe we're supposed to do it in a different way.

Don't assume it's time to bail out of your marriage because you've "lost that lovin' feelin' and it's gone . . . gone . . . gone. . . ."[6] You don't need a divorce; you need to see things in a fresh way. Get a new perspective. Find some new ways to light the fire in your relationship! Make plans to go out on a date night. Do it in a big way. Maybe even make plans to have a getaway together. Before you say you can't afford to, consider that maybe you can't afford not to.

Not only that, but maybe you've been waiting for your spouse to change when what you need to do is make a change in yourself. Think about what you can do to make yourself more appealing and attractive to your spouse.

> Sometimes God wants you to keep doing what you're doing, but he wants you to do it in a different way.

Most people make changes after a divorce to attract someone new. They lose weight and start looking and being their best. I always wonder why didn't they do that when they were married? If they had made those changes before the divorce, they may not be divorced!

Don't assume that when your experience at work gets stale it's a sign you must change your job or find another career. It could be a sign that you're supposed to keep doing what you're doing but in a different way, with a new attitude or a new approach. It could mean it's time to implement some new methods and fresh ideas.

I see people at our church find new excitement just by doing what they do differently. It's amazing when someone who has been coming to church for a long time brings someone to church with him. It is the same church as it has been, but he experiences it through fresh eyes.

When people change where they sit in church or start serving on a new team, that can create a favor shift. They meet new people, experience new opportunities, and find themselves going home blessed because they made a shift. They're still coming to the same church, but they're coming in a different way.

When we do what we do in a different way, we can get different results.

A good friend of mine, Edward, was a two-sport athlete who received a scholarship to play college football. After he got out of college he began to gain weight. When he got married in 1978 he weighed 206 pounds, but by 2013 he had topped out at 325 pounds. I had heard him joke about his weight for years and knew he wanted to lose some, but like many people he never really made up his mind to do it.

On his thirty-fifth wedding anniversary in 2013, he set a goal to lose thirty-five pounds, and when that goal was accomplished, he didn't stop. He continued making progress, and a year after he began his weight-loss journey, he'd lost a total of 119 pounds and was back to what he'd weighed when he got married.

In addition to feeling great, Edward has experienced several health benefits, lowered the amount of medication he takes, and—my favorite— instead of being out of breath after climbing a flight of stairs, he now is running 5K and longer races. Now one of his greatest joys is that he has a high level of energy and can play more with his grandkids. He's even become a health coach and is helping others who want to lose weight and learn good health habits.

In a recap of his journey, Edward wrote, "There was just one thing that clicked in me . . . I was ready and decided to do it!" Today Edward's health is better, his confidence is stronger, and he's enjoying his life more because he went from thinking about it to doing something about it. Edward's story proves that a shift in you doesn't just benefit you; it benefits those around you.

It must have been a wild and crazy episode when Simon's fishing nets were stretched to the breaking point. I imagine men yelling for help and shouting directions, and every muscle on board straining and stretching in an effort to draw more fish than they'd ever seen into the boat!

On a normal day, if they had hit a hot spot for fishing, Simon might have been tempted to keep the spot a secret. But this was not just a hot spot. This was an abundance that overflowed into the lives of all those who worked for Simon, as well as all those in the other boats.

Simon wasn't the only one who benefited from his internal shift; lots of other people also were blessed in the process. That's the way it is when we make the right shift in our attitudes and actions. Other people experience the benefit too.

Years ago, I started praying a prayer as I prepare to speak that goes like this: "God, help me help people." Sometimes I say it twenty-five or more times in the days leading up to the weekend. It helps me get other things off my mind and shift into the attitude I need to be a benefit to my listeners. Anytime we empty weighty things off our mind and take our thoughts off ourselves, the people around us benefit.

Charles Colson, a former aide to President Nixon, spent time in prison after his involvement in the Watergate scandal. When he was released from prison he could have lived a very private life—self-absorbed or embarrassed. Instead he decided to be obedient to what he sensed God was telling him to do, which involved a major shift in his life work and focus. The result was the beginning of Prison Fellowship, which is currently the world's largest prison outreach organization. Its programs reach prisoners, ex-prisoners, and families of prisoners throughout the United States and in 112 countries worldwide.

It can be a small shift or a major shift, but anytime we are obedient in making that shift, it blesses us and those around us.

## SHIFT YOUR MIND-SET

Sometimes the shift we need to make is to get our minds off the past and on to the future.

In the story of the Exodus, as the Israelites left Egypt, God ordered a shift to help his people leave the past and look to the future.

> The angel of God that had been leading the camp of Israel now shifted and got behind them. And the Pillar of Cloud that had been in front also shifted to the rear. (Exodus 14:19, MSG)

This *shift* created a separation between them and their past—a visual separation. This was God's way of saying, *I don't want you looking* behind *you; I want you to shift your attention to what's* ahead *of you.*

Maybe you're *living* with regrets of what you did or did not do: *I could have said this . . . Why did I do that? What was I thinking?*

Maybe you're still blaming yourself for a sin or failure or constantly reliving a season in your life that is over. Maybe you are stuck in a past relationship that ended, or maybe you are still angry with someone for something that happened a long time ago. When we replay the past, we miss out on the present and sabotage the future!

> *Sometimes the shift we need to make is to get our minds off the past and on to the future.*

God wants us to know the same thing he wanted the people of Israel to know: *I'll take care of the past; you just need to put your attention on the future!* If you've been looking too much to the past, change your mind-set. Shift your mind from where you've been to where you're going.

## SHIFT YOUR WORDS

We all face problems in life. Jesus said that in this world we would all have trouble, but nevertheless to be of good cheer (see John 16:33). In other words, even though trouble is inevitable we can choose to not let those problems get us down. And I also have found that when I do get down or feel discouraged, there's a second line of defense: the words I say.

Even if I've lost the battle in how I feel, I still have a chance to win if I say something better than how I feel. Our words have that much power to lift us up out of the funk and the junk we are feeling.

When I was in my early twenties, a pastor told me to get up every day and, no matter how I felt, to look in the mirror and say out loud, "I'm healthy, I'm happy, and I'm a Christian!" I took his advice and started saying this each morning, and I noticed a change in the way I felt when I headed out to face my day.

No one should always say how she feels—it's not wise. When you hear someone always sharing how she feels, she's not being smart, because words have so much influence on life. In fact, they can even bring death:

The tongue has the power of life and death,
   and those who love it will eat its fruit. (Proverbs 18:21)

You don't choose to be discouraged, but it's a good idea to choose your words when you are discouraged.

Feelings can be inaccurate. Feelings are fickle. So if you say what you feel in a heated moment, you may regret those words the rest of your life.

- The wrong words create strife; the right words bring peace.
- The wrong words tear down; the right words build up.
- The wrong words make a mountain; the right words move the mountain.
- The wrong words speak death; the right words give life.

The right words will sometimes be words that are completely opposite of what you feel.

I was watching a sports channel one night when I learned about a young man named Isaiah Austin. He was a rising basketball star on his way to a career in the NBA. Isaiah had been a fantastic college player at Baylor University before deciding to declare his eligibility for the 2014 NBA draft. During a physical just days before the draft, doctors diagnosed Isaiah with Marfan syndrome, a rare genetic disorder affecting the heart. Marfan syndrome can be successfully treated, but contact sports are out because of the danger of potentially fatal damage to the aorta.

It was a stunning blow to a young man who had worked hard all his life only to have his dreams suddenly taken away by circumstances beyond his control.

I was intrigued about Isaiah and learned during a online search that he is an active and engaged Christ follower.

During the week of the 2014 NBA draft, Isaiah used social media to express that only God knows the plans he has for his life. He shared on Instagram, "God, I put ALL my faith and ALL my trust into you! Jeremiah 29:11: 'For I know the plans I have for you,' declares the Lord. 'Plans to prosper you and not to harm you, plans to give you hope and a future.' God is good all the time! No matter what the situation! #facts #NewBeginnings."

The seven-foot-one Christian encouraged his followers to tune in to the announcement on ESPN, then tweeted thanks for the outpouring of support he received after the news spread.

"I would love to thank *EVERYONE* who has reached out to me. Toughest days of my life. But not the last! Life goes on. *GOD IS STILL GREAT!*"

The former Baylor center was able to live out part of his dream when he heard commissioner Adam Silver call his name as a ceremonial pick between the fifteenth and sixteenth picks.

I have no doubt that Isaiah will succeed. His choice of words has already set his course in the right direction.

It might seem like a small thing, but right words create a shift in us and open us up to experience all that God has for us. We don't proclaim God's goodness with the idea that we won't have disappointments or experience struggles in our lives. We proclaim God's goodness in the midst of our disappointments and struggles in life.

Favor is not about God giving us immunity from life—from adversity and problems. Favor is about God giving us an advantage in life when facing those challenges.

## SOMETHING WAS HAPPENING . . . WHEN NOTHING WAS HAPPENING

When our church was looking for a place to open a Champions Centre in Bellevue, Washington, we couldn't get a break! Commercial buildings were at a 90 percent occupancy rate and nothing we tried worked.

When we found one place we were excited about, the neighbors didn't want us there and filed a petition to keep us out. They protested so vigorously at a meeting at the courthouse that afterward the mayor apologized to us for their bad behavior.

The city officials expressed regret and assured us they would like to have a Champions Centre in Bellevue, but nothing was working out. At that time, the permit process was taking years for a new building, and we couldn't find a piece of land anyway!

Then, literally overnight, everything changed. There was a definite shift, a holy shift. It was like God said, *This is the time and this is the place!* Everything started going our way. Our Realtor called and said a builder had all his permits approved but needed a tenant. We checked out the location and it was amazing! The property was situated near a strategic intersection of two interstate highways. The builder was willing to adjust his plans if the city would agree to modifications. We approached the city of Bellevue and asked if we could customize the plans for the inside of the building to be our church instead of an office building. This provided an opportunity for the mayor and city council to help us. They put the contractor's change request on a fast track, and we had a building permit and were ready to go in less than ninety days.

Our plan was a lease with the option to buy, but that purchase plan was delayed due to the economic downturn in 2007. However, along with the downturn came a huge drop in interest rates. As I said earlier, everything was going our way. Talk about *favor!*

However, believe me, it didn't feel like favor every step of the way, but the years of delay proved to be incredibly beneficial to our church. Not only did our local bank want to lend us money to buy the new building, but it also offered us an advantageous refinancing package on our Tacoma property that ended up saving us about one-third on our monthly mortgage payment.

The delays had been difficult. But at the time I could not have imagined how much was really happening when it felt like nothing was happening. This reminds me of the promise that God watches over his word to perform it (see Jeremiah 1:12), which means God is waiting for the perfect opportunity for his written promises to be performed in our lives.

• • •

Our daughter Jodi's dream was to play college basketball. As a parent, I not only loved watching her play but a college scholarship was definitely my idea of a blessing! She worked hard, got the interest of several schools around the nation, and ended up with a four-year, full-ride scholarship to Western Washington University. It was a dream come true, and she was excited to play for a great program and coach.

The joy began to fade as reality set in. It was hard for her to go from being a star in high school to being ninth off the bench on a roster of nine talented players. Not only was she not playing much but the two other freshmen quit by December, leaving her as the only newbie.

There were many discouraging moments and nights when she cried herself to sleep, feeling lonely and frustrated. She kept shifting her mind back to the right place, and I'll never forget when she texted me the message that said, "Dad, I'm in the starting lineup tonight." She had a terrific game, scoring twenty-eight points, and never looked back. She went on to enjoy a great college career and helped her team get to the postseason play-offs every year. She also graduated with honors as part of Sigma Iota Epsilon (a national honor society for top students in business).

What might have happened if Jodi had given in to her feelings and allowed her thoughts to shift in a negative direction? Words do matter!

If you're in a season of life where it feels like everything is in a holding pattern, stay true to your course and don't give up on your dream. *Just because you can't see something happening doesn't mean that nothing is happening.* It's in those times where you can't see what God is doing that God is preparing you for something and something for you.

At the right time, in due season, a shift will happen, and you will see the answer to your prayers.

# Favor Forecasts

For the LORD God is a sun and shield;
the LORD bestows favor and honor.

—PSALM 84:11

When Sheila and I moved to the Northwest, our congregation was small and so was our family budget. As a treat, one of our favorite activities for a date was to eat at a restaurant on the waterfront. The only small problem was that we couldn't afford to actually eat there. So we would go sit on the patio and share a dessert.

As we sat and enjoyed the incredible water view, waiters would pass by with entrées that looked and smelled so good that we wanted to grab the food off their trays. I remember telling Sheila, "Someday we will eat a full meal here!" Eventually, we were able to do that, and to this day when we are there, I remember the past, when eating our fill was something we could only talk about.

In other words, way back then I was a prophet!

Do you realize that you are a prophet too—that you speak prophetically every day? Maybe you need a minute to digest that statement because you might not believe that what you say is prophetic.

The word *prophecy* conjures up all kinds of images in our mind. In fact when we hear the word *prophet*—depending on our religious background and experiences—it might make us think of an Old Testament fire-breathing man declaring God's anger. Or we might see a preacher wearing a white suit with a big Bible in hand who holds crusades and revival meetings across the country. Or the image might be of a mystical person like a fortune-teller or palm reader who seems to have a window that reveals the future.

What most people don't realize is that all of us have and speak with a prophetic voice. You may not think of yourself as having this "gift," but chances are you've actually given yourself credit for being a prophet. I'm referring to the times when in retrospect you've said things such as: "I knew this was going to happen." "I knew we were on the right track." "I knew I shouldn't trust him." "I knew we had a lot in common the minute we met." What you were saying is, "I saw this working out a particular way before it actually happened!"

> *Forecast favor according to your faith, not your feelings or fears.*

In fact, it's possible you've prophesied something in the last few hours. You might have said something like, "We're going to have a great time when we get together." Or "I don't see anything good coming out of it." Or "It's all going to work out fine." Or "I know it's not going to be easy." Can you hear the prophetic insight in all of those common phrases?

We're constantly talking about something we sense or know about the future with some certainty of what's going to happen. So we all speak prophetic words in one way or another. But instead of calling this "prophetic," we call it thoughts, feelings, speculation, or assumptions.

In a related fashion, forecasting favor is using your voice to predict favor in your future.

My goal in this chapter is not to have you walking around telling people you are about to prophesy, because that will get you on the "strange and scary list" real quick. My goal is to help you see that you do prophesy and to encourage you to use this opportunity in everyday life to align yourself with God's plans for your future. I want you to forecast according to your *faith,* not your *feelings* or *fears.*

When we use our prophetic voice to predict God's goodness, we activate his will over our emotions. Since we're going to speak about the future, why not refer to it in full confidence of God's favor on it? Why not say, "God is with me. God is for me. God's plans for me are good!"? Let's say something like this:

> "For I know the plans I have for you," declares the LORD, "plans
> to prosper you and not to harm you, plans to give you hope and a
> future." (Jeremiah 29:11)

You don't need to speak in some hyped-up or strange tone of spiritual arrogance but in your own natural, everyday way of conversing. Keep it real, but keep it courageous, so when you refer to life's challenges and troubles, also include words of confidence in God's goodness and favor.

In my book *Forces That Form Your Future,* the major concern I addressed is the tendency of people to assume they have little or no part to play in their future. This is a mistake.

As an athlete, I always wanted to be in the game. In high-school football, I played both offense and defense because I hated being on the sideline. If I was out of the game I knew I couldn't impact what was happening on the field.

Forecasting favor is how we stay on the field and influence the game of life. It's us playing our part. It's our way of being on the side of God's favor in everything we do.

## BE A PROPHET OF GOOD—NOT A PROPHET OF DOOM

The massive media coverage of tragic events has a way of making us assume that we live in the worst of times. But even if it's the worst of times in some ways, it's the best of times in other ways. My point is that the world is neither more nor less evil now than ever before. Evil is contained by good and matched by good. Good is alive and well because God is alive and well. God has not forsaken the world; God loves the world.

Don't allow the daily reports of evil to cause you to assume that the evil of the world is slowly overtaking the good. In fact it is just the opposite! You have every reason to assume the future is a place of promise and a place of hope. Rather than letting the uncertainty of the future cause you to worry and fear, shift your thoughts to the obvious presence of good around you.

The good you see and hear every day may not be making the news in your city, but you can make sure it's on the headlines of your heart and mind.

You can also predict it will be there tomorrow, and you can forecast it in your future! Goodness is not going away. The earth is not being swept away by evil. Good will prevail. Light will prevail over darkness. Blessing and favor will continue and grow in the believer's life generationally. The seeds of kindness, generosity, and encouragement that you sow today are going to show up in tomorrow's harvest!

So don't be afraid to forecast favor in your future. The entirety of Psalm 37 is filled with the language of forecasting favor. I encourage you to read it slowly and savor every word. Here's a brief sample:

Do not fret because of those who are evil
    or be envious of those who do wrong;
for like the grass they will soon wither,
    like green plants they will soon die away.

Trust in the LORD and do good;
    dwell in the land and enjoy safe pasture.

Take delight in the LORD,

   and he will give you the desires of your heart. (verses 1–4)

Forecasting favor is not speculation or a goofy wish list turned into a word from God.

If you're going into business, for sure do your research in the market. Form a business strategy. Don't just aimlessly speculate and assume that favor will cover bad investments and unwise decisions.

If you're going to buy a home, make sure you have good inspectors check out the structure and safety of the house. Don't assume you can buy the house and skip due diligence because you have favor.

Speculation is where people get messed up. They speculate based on their human instincts, assumptions, greed, fears, and biases. On the other hand, prophetic audacity is not human speculation or words of manipulation but rather sound and biblical forecasting of the future.

> *It's easy to confuse what we want with what God wants for us.*

I agree that it's easy to confuse what we want with what God wants for us. A desire can be so strong that some people conclude it must be God's will when it may just be their own cravings. When this happens those people misuse God's name to validate doing what they want to do. They tell other people things like, "God told me to leave my job" or "God told me to go to a different church."

Single and desperate people have sometimes said to someone that "God told me we're supposed to get married." When people say things like that it's not a prophetic word; it's a primal urge! A lady in our church looked back at a guy who told her that and said, "God hasn't said a word about it to me!"

I've witnessed my share of manipulation by people who claimed to have a word from God for my life or for our church. People have said to me that if I didn't hear or obey the word they gave me, something tragic would happen to me or my family. Fortunately, they survived my ferocious flurry of right jabs and left hooks! (At least that's what I saw myself doing for a moment in my mind.) But seriously, this sort of manipulation and abuse has given a bad name to the word *prophecy* and caused people to practice discretion when sensing a directional clue from God.

One way to discern is to know that New Testament prophecy is for building up people not tearing them down. Its primary purpose is to encourage people, in God's ways. So when it comes to specific directional words that you sense God may be saying, it is always best to leave lots of room for them being completely wrong!

On the other hand, when it comes to forecasting favor over your own future, there's no risk of being wrong. Be bold. Be audacious! Speak God's will and favor over your life while also staying away from speculations.

Forecasting favor is using specific words related to where you are right now. **For example, a single man's forecast of favor should sound like this:** "I know God has a great plan for my life. God's got the *right person* picked out, and at the right time, she will come into my life. Until then, I'm confident and focused on where God has me right now."

**In marriage the forecast of favor declares love and friendship.** It declares the certainty of forever. It speaks of marriage as getting more fun and more fulfilling with the passing of time. It uses words to anticipate that the best of times is ahead. It says, "We will have fun when we . . . We will be in a position then to . . . We will go on that trip . . . We will help the church do . . . We will spoil our grandkids together."

**In business the forecast of favor declares open doors.** It proclaims the favor of the connections with the right people at the right time. It predicts that the right doors are opening up. It speaks financial strength and increase into your business and personal life.

**In parenting the forecast of favor calls our children blessed and highly favored.** It speaks greatness over them and their future. When Jodi was in preschool Sheila started the habit of leading Jodi in putting on the armor of God before she faced her day. That happened all through Jodi's young school life. Every morning before Jodi got out of the car at school, she would armor up! Now that's how Jodi starts the day with her son Kyan. Words like that help parents and children step boldly into the day.

**In all of life the forecast of favor helps us to not be anxious or worried.** It helps us avoid negative assumptions based in fear and creates assurance in our minds that God has plans to prosper us and bless us in our future.

As the Bible says, when you get up in the morning, both life and death are in front of you (see Deuteronomy 30:15). That means you will decide whether you're going to proclaim life, blessing, and favor or proclaim negativity, discouragement, and death. Scripture tells us to "choose life, so that you and your children may live" (verse 19).

> *Words are carriers of God's plan and activate God's will.*

Notice that God doesn't say, "I choose for you to walk in life today, whether you like it or not!" No! God's tells *us* to choose life, but then he leaves the actual choice up to us. There are other paths we can walk on, but the path of favor is a chosen path. And the most significant and powerful way we choose that path is by our words.

It's a courageous move and a game changer in the outcome of your circumstances when you choose your words well. At first it may seem presumptuous to place this sort of weightiness on words. The idea that words are carriers of God's plan and actually activate God's will places huge significance on them. But I'm not making this up! Look at what these verses say about the creative power of words:

- "Gracious words are a honeycomb, sweet to the soul and healing to the bones" (Proverbs 16:24).

- "Through the blessing of the upright a city is exalted" (Proverbs 11:11).
- "From the fruit of their lips people enjoy good things" (Proverbs 13:2).

What if "gracious words" are not spoken? What if "the blessing" is not proclaimed?

If our words are negative, what does that mean the fruit of our lips will be? What if we speak despair and defeat? Is it possible that what God wills as his favor in a person's life or even in a city or a church cannot be realized because of a person's failure to proclaim it? Absolutely!

Don't let that be the case in your life. Say words of favor to keep favor flowing into your world.

## KEEP YOUR FORECAST THE SAME
## REGARDLESS OF THE WEATHER

In *The War of Art*, author Steven Pressfield says that we all have two lives: the life we live and the unlived *life within us*. The only way for the unlived life to be lived is to engage the resistance that is certain to be between us and the unlived life—our future hopes and dreams.

No question—for most of us, God's will and favor are easier to proclaim when things are good in our lives. When you get that new job or promotion, when your relationships are in sync, when you are moving to a much-needed bigger house—these are times when it's easy to look around and see God's blessings and proclaim his favor.

However, when you just got notice that your job is being terminated or your insurance won't cover the hospital bill or your nine-year-old is being held back due to what the teacher described as a learning disability, it's much easier to turn on the sad country western music and have yourself a pity party.

*But that's the most important time to keep favor in the forecast.*

I'm not suggesting that you can forecast favor and see the weather change immediately. I am suggesting that you keep your forecast the same regardless of the weather.

Scripture says, "Let the weak say, I am strong" (Joel 3:10, KJV). It doesn't say, "Let the weak admit it."

If this seems to you like a slap in the face of transparent authenticity, I understand. It might also seem counterintuitive. But this rally cry is neither of those. It's a reference to what the writer Joel saw when he looked ahead to the future when courageous people of God would stand against the oppression of their enemies. He saw people who would not allow their weakness to excuse them from battle. He saw people who would not let old age hinder them from engaging in the fight for their freedom. He saw people who would rise to the occasion when they had their backs against the wall. Rather than folding under the pressure, they would tap into the strength that comes from God by proclaiming their strength in times of weakness.

I understand the need for us, in an effort to encourage one another, to be honest about our struggles. I've found that I help people by letting them know I don't always have my Sunday smile on. But you can be authentic about challenges and weaknesses and still proclaim your confidence.

The apostle Paul said, "I can do all things through Christ who strengthens me" (Philippians 4:13, NKJV). What was he doing? He was proclaiming the favor advantage he had on his life. He said, "I can . . . through Christ." This kind of proclamation is not just hyped-up propaganda, and it's much more than some form of self–pep talk! This is proclaiming what Jesus has proclaimed . . . *the unending year of the Lord's favor* (see Luke 4:18–19). It's declaring God's goodness, blessings, kindness, and protection over my life in every season.

King David was a great example of forecasting favor in the face of resistance. After he had listened to the threats of Goliath and surveyed the situation, he stood before King Saul seeking permission to fight the giant. There in the presence of Saul we begin to hear his prophetic audacity: "The LORD who rescued me from the paw of the lion and the paw of the bear will rescue me from the hand of this Philistine" (1 Samuel 17:37).

To some these may have seemed the words of an overambitious young man, but David was prophesying according to his faith. He knew God's promises and foresaw the Lord giving him and the nation of Israel the victory they both needed that day.

Later as David approached Goliath for battle, the giant cursed him and hurled insults at him, but David remained unshakeable. He was not intimidated by the circumstances that seemed to be stacked against him. Again he spoke prophetically with great audacity about the victory God was going to bring:

> You come against me with sword and spear and javelin, but I come against you in the name of the LORD Almighty, the God of the armies of Israel, whom you have defied. This day the LORD will deliver you into my hands, and I'll strike you down and cut off your head. This very day I will give the carcasses of the Philistine army to the birds and the wild animals, and the whole world will know that there is a God in Israel. All those gathered here will know that it is not by sword or spear that the LORD saves; for the battle is the LORD's, and he will give all of you into our hands. (verses 45–47)

Go, David! Call it before it happens! Proclaim in advance that at the end of the battle the Lord will make you victorious!

What victory awaits in your life today? What battle is waiting for you to partner with and proclaim God's favor?

A few things we can learn from David's victory that day:

- First, God didn't spare David from a fight.
- Second, God did not take out Goliath without David. He took out Goliath *through* David. The resistance to your progress is an enemy you must engage. God will bring success *through* you.
- Third, David didn't wait until the battle was over to proclaim his victory. He forecasted favor *before* and *during* the battle.

There's no way for you to know what kind of resistance will stand up to oppose your progress, but God's Word promises that "no weapon forged against you will prevail" (Isaiah 54:17). Resistance is certain. Adversity will come. When it does, be like David—stand up and use your prophetic voice.

Let your words be the words of a winner.

Have the confidence of a champion.

Talk about the victories coming your way.

Proclaim good things over your future.

Declare God's blessings on your tomorrows.

Speak life over your legacy.

Proclaim that your best days are ahead of you!

Enjoy the good things God has promised!

# Don't Settle in Spain  (18)

Don't settle. As with all matters of the
heart, you'll know when you find it.

—STEVE JOBS

I don't think we heirs of Abraham were ever supposed to end up as couch potatoes. Sitting in one spot can feel so comfortable. But there must be a better way to live.

Christopher Columbus, the great renowned explorer, grew up in Spain at a time when Spain was very proud of the fact that they were the last point of solid land for sailors going westward. When travelers arrived in Spain by boat (usually from Africa), the first things they would see as they entered the strait leading to the port of Spain were two large pillars on each side of the canal inscribed with Spain's national motto. The motto in Latin was *Ne Plus Ultra,* which means "No More Beyond." These same words showed up on Spain's flag and coins as well.

This message was one the nation took pride in and believed as their outlook on life. "No more beyond" was not considered to be negative in nature. It was mainly a reference to the geographical location of Spain in the world, as they knew it. Many people saw Spain as a major destination in that day because getting to Spain meant you had gone to the end of civilization and reached the ultimate place on earth. There was now *no more beyond.*

The effect this had on people, though, was that they settled there.

Since there was nothing beyond, why *think* beyond there? Or *dream* beyond there?

This is the message that young Christopher Columbus saw everywhere as he was growing up. It's how everyone thought. But it wasn't the message Christopher believed. In fact, he put everything he had into the idea that there was something beyond. That belief is what inspired and fueled his vision. He raised support and the backing of the king to sail west into uncharted waters.

Everything changed in Spain after Columbus discovered the New World. Spain entered what was called the Age of Discovery. The national motto changed too. The king ordered that the "Ne" be dropped so that the new motto was *Plus Ultra*. Flags were changed and they engraved new coins with the phrase *Plus Ultra,* which means "More Beyond." The nation embraced the reality of more beyond where they were.

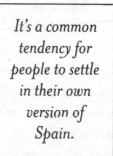

*It's a common tendency for people to settle in their own version of Spain.*

Sadly, I have found that it's a common tendency for people to settle in their own version of Spain. The no-more-beyond mentality falls far short of what God has in mind for their lives. They get to a certain point and begin to believe there's nothing greater left for them. They accept something far less than God's bigger, greater plans for their lives.

Men and women settle. Old and young settle. People of all ethnicities and economic statuses settle. Believers and unbelievers settle. Businesses and churches settle. Even while people are active, they settle. Just because people go to work, clean the house, balance the checkbook, and go to the kids' games doesn't mean they haven't settled in their own version of Spain. Life may go on for them, but it's still *Ne Plus Ultra*.

## THERE IS A DIFFERENCE BETWEEN SETTLED PRIORITIES AND SETTLED PASSION

Don't get me wrong; being settled can be good in some ways. When people say, "I'm going to settle down," they typically mean something positive—like "settle down and devote my time to my marriage and family." Most people realize it is good to be settled geographically and to put down roots in a community for the sake of family stability. Scripture says

> Settled passion will hinder God's favor.

it is good to get planted in a church (see Psalm 92:13), which is a form of being settled. So, God has a right place and a right people for us, and when we are in that place and with those people, God wants us to live committed to those people and that place. I describe this as being settled in *priorities*.

When priorities like faith, family, and fitness are settled, they serve as a strong foundation for a life of favor. When priorities are settled you'll live your life, form your habits, and make your decisions from a place of confidence.

When we're settled in our priorities we carry them forward day after day, week after week, and year after year. They are what matter most to us and serve as a gauge to measure our success.

God's favor is on people whose priorities are settled.

I don't think it's the same way with passion, though. In fact, settled passion will hinder God's favor.

Passion doesn't mean you always jump up singing in the morning. If that were the case, I would fail the passion test every day! Neither is passion always happy, smiley, and carefree.

Sometimes passion is burdened or intense. Sometimes passion is high energy and sometimes passion is laid-back. The emotions and expressions of passion vary, but the one thing that's constant with passion is *drive*.

Passionate people are unsettled. Their drive causes them to always believe there is more. When you stop wanting more, thinking more, and expecting more, you're starting to settle.

And there's a deception that goes along with being settled: settled people don't think of themselves as having settled.

When people settle,

- they are not as interested in learning and trying new things;
- they usually stop taking good care of themselves physically;
- they no longer reach for things beyond their current grasp;
- they stop imagining and dreaming of things they want to do or experience in the future; and
- they generally have less fun and are unwilling to take risks.

Settling is just another way to miss out on God's favor.


## THREE REASONS PEOPLE SETTLE

I want to familiarize you with some of the reasons for *Ne Plus Ultra* in a person's life, just in case you ever start seeing them in yourself:

*1. People settle when they get sentimentally attached to a past season of their life.*

    Sometimes people are supposed to stay *where* they have been, but nothing is supposed to stay *like* it has been. When people don't evolve with life and embrace change, they settle for a lifetime in what was meant to be a season.

    If you've had a setback recently or suffered the loss of a loved one, no one should fault you for having grief or discouragement in your life. But I want to encourage you to not let the temporary conditions of your life dictate a permanent perspective.

Imagine the challenge in this: after being freed from years of slavery, the Israelite people were sentimentally attached to and kept referring back to the place they came from. Moses had to lead them to keep looking forward to a new place and encourage them to not look back. He told them on several occasions to keep expecting the answer to their prayers and that God was about to bring them to a new place, a new season, and a greater day of joy in their lives.

2. *People settle in a place of relational wounds.*

In Genesis 11, Abraham's father, Terah, was on his way with his family to Canaan, which is where God planned for him to go and live. Terah had another son who died a premature death. Terah was on his way to Canaan, but he had to go through a place named Haran to get there. Rather than passing through, Terah settled in a city with the same name as the son he had lost.

I heard my friend Pastor Chris Hodges explain that we don't know for sure why Terah settled there. He wasn't supposed to. That wasn't God's plan. What we do know is that no father loses a son without heartache and grieving. Sons are supposed to outlive fathers. It is highly likely that Terah stopped and stayed in the city of Haran because he was grieving the loss of his son.

Eventually, God spoke to Abraham and he moved to Canaan. It is reasonable to assume that God had intended for Abraham and his family to be there all along, but his father had settled in Haran.

Relational wounds can be terribly debilitating, and many people settle in the place of a lost relationship. They allow themselves to linger mentally and emotionally in a place that God wants them to move beyond.

Or sometimes people choose to leave our lives. That can hurt. But when it happens, never ask them to stay. Just know that God has new and better relationships in mind for you. You're better off and will be a lot happier being with people who want to be with you.

When you are offended or wounded relationally, it may seem justified to nurse the wound, to rehearse the injustice. You may have a right and good reason to be hurt. But anger will eventually consume you, and bitterness will destroy you if you let it. The best thing to do is to forgive those people and move on.

Don't let yourself linger in the place of relational wounds and miss out on the future God has for you.

3. *People settle because where they are is "good enough" and they want to stay comfortable.*

So right about now, you may be thinking, *Kevin, settling isn't really that bad. Settled people can still enjoy a good life.* But just because someone makes the best of his life doesn't mean he's living his best life. "Good enough" is the enemy of "better than ever"!

Don't make the mistake of settling for good enough. Good enough is not your destiny! Are you aware that being comfortable is way overrated? The best things in life don't come when you're comfortable. In fact, being too comfortable can clog your arteries, soften your muscles, and make you weak and tired. Your body may want to settle and be comfortable, but that's not how you experience the healthiest and best life.

Ask any mom who's about to have a baby if she's comfortable. She may slap you for asking! She's very uncomfortable! You don't bring new life into the world by being comfortable.

When we think of our jobs, we don't think in terms of comfort. We know we can't earn a good living if we're focused on our comfort.

The place of "good enough" might sound tempting because it's more comfortable. But it's not the place God has for you. "Good enough" is not your destiny. Ignore the signs that say "no more beyond." That message is a lie that wants us to settle and miss out on all that God has beyond where we are right now.

## DRIFTING IS NOT A DIRECTION

If settling is not such a great idea, drifting is just as bad. The Christian life is about *going somewhere with God*. How cool is that!

Here is what the author of Hebrews wrote about drifting: "We must pay the most careful attention, therefore, to what we have heard, so that we do not drift away" (2:1).

Notice the word chosen: *drift*. Sometimes what we hear about God seems too good to be true. That he loves us just as we are—our faults, our baggage, our issues. That he forgives us, heals us, helps us, blesses us, wants the best for us. We hear that message at church on Sunday and get so encouraged by the incredible promises of God for our lives.

But then Monday rolls around, and we step back into a faulty world with all of its challenges. That's when the drift starts to happen. We start to draw on our old data, and before we know what's happened, we're drifting back to a more reasonable idea of God—one that's not so grand.

One that's not so hard to believe. One that downsizes the goodness of God so we can factor in the hardship of life.

Have you ever been on a boat that's just drifting? When I was a kid one of our favorite things to do was to get on a pontoon boat that our friends owned and go out into the middle of the lake and swim. Sometimes we didn't bother to drop anchor, and it was amazing how far the boat would drift because of wind and currents. It's the same way with our soul: the unanchored soul will drift.

We live in a windy world: questions, assumptions, doubts, worries, other people's opinions, philosophies, and bad experiences all add up to . . . *windy* at work, school, and even at home. These winds can cause you to drift into disappointment, discouragement, negativity, and anxiety. The unanchored soul is subject to the winds and currents of life.

I don't know about you, but I'm so amazed at how quickly people change their perspectives on life. Sometimes we find ourselves sailing in the open waters of faith and confidence on Sunday, and then we find ourselves drifting back into waters of worry and

> *The unanchored soul will drift.*

fear on Monday. One moment you're feeling good about yourself, and then that person at work, who always has the latest of everything, shows you his newest tech toy, and you are reminded that you are still using an old cell phone that's so big it won't fit in your pocket!

One thing you can be sure of is that no matter your age, gender, background, or status, an unanchored soul will drift. And the only way we can avoid the drift into a low-grade, compromised, downsized version of God is to drop anchor in God's goodness.

Let's look at what the author said to the Hebrews who kept rationalizing away what they thought was the too-good-to-be-true goodness of God. He first told them to pay close attention to the good news they had first heard so they wouldn't drift away from it. Then they learned what the anchor was that would keep their souls from drifting: "We have this hope as an anchor for the soul, firm and secure. . . . Where our forerunner, Jesus, has entered on our behalf" (6:19–20).

The author is  saying in so many words, "Don't reason away what you have learned; even though it seems too good to be true, it's true! God is really that good! He sent his Son, Jesus, as a once-and-for-all sacrifice for our sins. Don't drift back to trying to perform your way into God's favor. Put your hope in God's too-good-to-be-true-but-it-is plan of salvation."

# The Unfinished Works of God (19)

He who began a good work in you will
carry it on to completion.

—PHILIPPIANS 1:6

It's what you learn after you know it all
that counts.

—JOHN WOODEN

God's favor for us will last forever.

I was looking through some pictures of the works of Michelangelo when it occurred to me that many of his famous works are incomplete. There are statues where one eye is finished and the other eye is missing the pupil. There are statues where body parts are missing. One arm is halfway done or a leg stops at the knee. I guess I've always assumed that these pieces were halfway done on purpose to give an artistic effect. The reality is that oftentimes Michelangelo and other artists would get bored with a project or would be hired for a different job, leaving the one they were working on incomplete.

Philippians 1:6 refers to the unfinished works of God and tells us to be confident of this: "He who began a good work in you will carry it on to completion." God has some unfinished works in your life right now that look like the unfinished works of Michelangelo. Something's missing. Something's incomplete. There may even be things you look at and see no way that something good can come of them. They may look now just like big messes.

> Sometimes God has to make us bigger on the inside before he can bring increase on the outside.

I want to encourage you and remind you that unlike Michelangelo, God's not dead and God's not done! God wants you to know that even though some things in your life look like unfinished works of art, the Artist is still at work! He's still doing his creative and brilliant work in your life and in your family's lives.

There are two kinds of unfinished works of God:

First, there's the work he's doing *in you:* "He who began a good work in you" (Philippians 1:6).

Then, there's the work he's doing *through you:* "We are God's handiwork, created in Christ Jesus to do good works, which God prepared in advance for us to do" (Ephesians 2:10).

These are both current, moment-by-moment works of God's grace and favor.

Sometimes God has to make us bigger on the inside before he can bring increase on the outside. This was the case with Christopher Columbus. As told in a legendary story, Columbus's inspiration to venture out of Spain was most likely connected to the day that one of his ancestors, Stephen Columbus, saved the life of a Spanish monk named Ramon Lull. Lull was preaching the gospel on the African coast when he was beaten and lay near death. Stephen was one of the men who picked him up, treated his wounds, and attempted to bring him home to Spain.

As they were crossing the Mediterranean, Lull lay in the bow of the boat and, in one of his final moments of life, pointed his finger westward over the horizon and said, "Beyond this sea which washes this continent we know lies another continent we've never seen . . . Send men there, send men there!"

These words lived on in the minds of the men who rescued him and were passed down through generations to a young Christopher, who became convinced that God had chosen him to spread the gospel to the land beyond the seas. It took years of appealing in the royal courts before Columbus received permission to actually set sail. But he refused to give up because he believed there was *more beyond* Spain.

God worked all those years *in him* causing him to think beyond the sea, to unknown continents. For all those years God was at work in him because of what he wanted to do *through him*. Although he was surrounded with signs that said "No More Beyond," God was using audacious prophetic words passed down through his family to make him bigger on the inside than the messages surrounding him.

God works *in us* first. If we listen closely, we'll see that he is at work in you and me right now. He's telling us he's not finished working in us and through us. His incomplete work is not his final work.

## KEEP YOUR WHOLE HEART IN THE UNFINISHED WORK

Don't be discouraged by the way something looks right now. When something's half-finished, it lacks the clarity of a complete work. When something's half-finished, it can make you wonder what is happening or not happening. It often leads to speculation, assumptions, and uncertainty.

When a cake is half-baked, it doesn't look that great.

When we drive by a construction site we might say, "I wonder what they are building there?" Because that's how half-finished projects affect us. They cause us to question what it is or why it is. It can be tempting to judge it before it's done, but we know it's not wise to judge a half-baked cake or a construction project while work is in process.

In the area where I live there's currently a major bridge under construction, and it doesn't look safe to drive on right now because it's not finished.

As parents, when we first see the ultrasound of an unborn child, we're not worried by what body parts are underdeveloped, because we know the creative process still needs time.

I remember as a kid going on a school field trip to the Chrysler auto plant and seeing the assembly line. There's no way anyone would want to try to drive a half-built car!

The incomplete works of God are the same as the half-baked cake, the unfinished construction project, the underdeveloped child, and the unfinished car. They can look odd when you're looking at them.

If you're a parent who raised your children in church and now that they are older they don't even want to attend church, that feels odd to you. You've probably lost sleep wondering why they turned out this way.

If you're a single person who has been putting God first, staying away from the social scene so popular with your friends at work or school, and not seeing any sign of that right person coming along, you may sometimes wonder, *Why? What's wrong with me?*

Maybe you've worked hard on your education and prepared diligently for your career, but no doors are opening up in your chosen field.

| *Favor will have the final word!* |
|---|

If so, you may be thinking it's really odd that you have put in all this work and now have no opportunities to use the skills you acquired. Why hasn't God opened a door for you? But sometimes roads have to close and things have to get worse before they get better.

It's the same way when God is doing a work in us or through us. You may have heard it said before, "Delayed doesn't mean denied!" The work he's doing may require your patience. The only way to respond during that season is to embrace the delay, hold on to your joy, and remain confident that God will continue the work to completion.

So be confident and continue doing what you know to do. I'm not talking about just going through the motions with no sense of expectation. I'm talking about keeping your expectations strong so that he who began a work will complete it (see Philippians 1:6).

There's a verse in Acts 2 that says the disciples "devoted themselves to [their] teaching and to fellowship, to the breaking of bread and to prayer" (verse 42).

First Thessalonians 5:17 says, "Pray continually." There are some things we are to do and never stop doing. There's power when you continue and never stop doing what you know to do, regardless of what is happening in your life:

- Continue in prayer.
- Continue attending and being a part of God's church.
- Continue in giving your tithes and offerings to God.
- Continue to proclaim God's goodness.
- Continue to be thankful.
- Continue to look for and expect God's favor in your life.

When you get discouraged, remind yourself that God's not finished. Favor will have the final word! Keep your whole heart in the unfinished work.

## GOD'S FAVOR LIVES IN OUR GREATEST HOPES AND DREAMS

So much of what has happened in history was once beyond imagination, which shows how limits in our minds can create lids on our lives. Here are some examples of what some people once said that must have seemed reasonable at the time, but looking back it is clear that the limitations were in their thinking, not in reality.

- Simon Newcomb, an astronomer in 1902, said, "Flight by machines heavier than air is unpractical and insignificant, if not utterly impossible."
- Grover Cleveland, president of the United States, said, "Sensible and responsible women do not want to vote."
- Harry Warner of Warner Bros. Pictures in 1927 said, "Who wants to hear actors talk anyway?"
- Ken Olsen, president of Digital Equipment Corporation, said in 1977, "There is no reason for any individual to have a computer in his home."

Limits are broken and lids are lifted by people who have great hope and big dreams.

- In a time when segregation was the norm, Rosa Parks broke a racial barrier by sitting in and refusing to move from the "whites only" section of the bus.
- For years the four-minute mile seemed unreachable, and then in 1954 a young student at Oxford University, Roger Bannister, stunned the world by breaking the four-minute barrier.
- In this generation, Bill Gates and Steve Jobs have both led barrier breakthroughs in technology that have revolution-ized the world.
- Chuck Yeager, an American test pilot, defied fear and doubts to become the first human to break the sound barrier.

**If we want to experience all that God has for us, we need to keep our minds open to the possibilities that seem impossible.** Rather than accepting the self-imposed limits that a lot of people place on themselves, we have to keep imagining the possibilities and believe that with God all things are possible.

My prayer for you is that you're fully convinced that God's favor is for you. Don't waste a prayer trying to convince God to give you his favor! Know that he's already committed to supply you with a lifetime of favor, and thank him for it! Remember, your hopes and dreams draw on that favor. God's favor is not needed or drawn on when people are settled and satisfied. God's favor is in places where we use our faith to stretch and reach beyond our current conditions and comfort zones.

> *Limits are broken and lids are lifted by people who have big dreams.*

If you're in the young or middle years of your life, your mind-set has to stay in a place of expectation that you will see frontiers that no previous generation has seen. Embrace the idea that the sky is the limit and this is the day of unprecedented opportunity.

The opportunities this age has birthed are limitless. The world is primed for new breakthroughs in medicine, arts, technology, and business. The greatest churches are yet to be built. The greatest songs are still unwritten. This generation has a huge opportunity to see good overcome evil and knowledge overtake ignorance.

No generation has had the opportunity of this generation!

Don't embrace this thinking just for you but also for your children. It is so easy to get entrenched in the up-close perspective of parenting and lose touch with the bigger picture of your children's lives. Keep adjusting your mind-set and elevating out of the daily details of hair combing, tooth brushing, bike riding, loud talking, hair pulling, and fist fighting so you have glimpses of your children as destined for greatness and legendary achievements. Speak God's favor over them and their future.

If on the other hand you're in the second half of your life and you've experienced a great deal of God's favor on your life, then your mind needs to be on the idea that there's no quota on God's favor. His favor is like a waterfall that never stops flowing and that lasts a lifetime. If you are still alive, he has more favor in mind for you. Don't get stuck in the "good ole days" mentality and miss out on what God has for you today and tomorrow.

Think beyond where you are. Keep reminding yourself to avoid limiting thoughts. Remind yourself to not settle in any version of your Spain but to keep believing that God has more for you! God's plan for you is that you will always experience his never-ending, ongoing favor.

*His favor lasts a lifetime!*

# Closing

I opened this book with two questions that I asked you to carefully consider. The first one had to do with God and the good things he promises us.

The second question was more personal: What do you think God thinks about you?

I pray that this book has convinced you that we have an incredibly generous Father who has set us up to receive an abundance of his ongoing, unlimited, unending favor!

I also trust you have a deeper awareness of how much your heavenly Father cares about you and, like any good dad, wants good things and the very best life for you!

As a father, I can relate to this—constantly wanting the absolute best for my daughter, Jodi, and now for my grandson, Kyan. I'm sure if you're a parent you are dialed in to that same natural and powerful desire to see your children and grandchildren have the best life this side of heaven.

But while God is perfect in all his ways, I'm still a work in progress. Like the day I was trying to have a good time with Kyan and scared him out of his little wits—twice.

When Kyan was fifteen months old, I volunteered to look after him one day. I knew it would be fun to hang out with him, and it turned out to be an adventurous day with several new experiences.

With him strapped in the car seat, I decided to take him through a car wash. I didn't know it was his first time to watch all the brushes and rollers moving around us making loud noises. I watched as he leaned over and his eyes got really big. That's when his absolute freak-out happened!

When all the brushes and water came down across the car, around the sides, and right by his window, Kyan started looking for an escape hatch. I thought he was going to rip himself right out of that car seat! After it was all over, I finally got him calmed down and assured him everything was all right.

A bit later that same day, I was taking him through the mall when I realized that the Easter bunny was there. I thought, *Kyan is going to be excited to see the Easter bunny.* What I didn't know was that he had never seen the Easter bunny. But I was thinking, *Man, this is so fun. He's going to go see the Easter bunny.* And I'm not talking about a little Easter bunny; this was an Easter bunny on steroids—all eight feet of him!

I rolled Kyan up in his stroller and saw that the Easter bunny had nobody around him. He was standing in a little fenced-in area, and I thought, *This is my chance. Kyan's got him all to himself!* I pushed the stroller right up next to the Easter bunny's pen. Kyan was looking the other direction at something else, so I said, "Hey, look! Kyan, look!"

He turned around and it was absolute freak-out number two! Again, I'm not talking about a whimper and a few tears—this was an immediate bloody-murder scream. The child's lungs expanded to full capacity and he yelled at the top of his voice, while at the same time reaching for me and trying to eject out of that stroller.

It was so bad that later on I told his mom and dad that we had to go back to that Easter bunny, stay at a distance, and let Kyan watch. Otherwise, if this kid didn't get a better impression of what he'd seen, he was going to have a lifetime of nightmares of an eight-foot rabbit with huge floppy ears!

Anytime the territory of our lives is increasing it can be a scary experience!

Sometimes we're like Kyan was that day, afraid and unaware of his papa's commitment to provide for and protect him. I hope the next time you're feeling afraid, alone, in despair, or discouraged that you'll remember the words of Jesus that we started this book with:

> If you then, who are evil, know how to give good gifts to your children, how much more will your Father who is in heaven give good things to those who ask him! (Matthew 7:11, ESV)

We have every reason to remain confident in the goodness of God. He never leaves us nor forsakes us. He is always with us. He is always for us. His favor surrounds us like a shield. Not just yesterday or today but for a lifetime.

His favor is forever!

# Appendix 1: Bible Verses by Chapter

## BEGINNING

- If you then, who are evil, know how to give good gifts to your children, how much more will your Father who is in heaven give good things to those who ask him! (Matthew 7:11, ESV)

## CHAPTER 1: AM I SEEING CLEARLY?

- I remain confident of this: I will see the goodness of the LORD in the land of the living. (Psalm 27:13)
- Consequently, faith *comes* from hearing the message, and the message is heard through the word about Christ. (Romans 10:17)
- Every good thing given and every perfect gift is from above. (James 1:17, NASB)
- "Don't be afraid," the prophet answered. "Those who are with us are more than those who are with them." And Elisha prayed, "Open his eyes, LORD, so that he may see." Then the LORD opened the servant's eyes, and he looked and saw the hills full of horses and chariots of fire all around Elisha. (2 Kings 6:16–17)

## CHAPTER 2: NO MORE TURNING

- I will make an everlasting covenant with them: I will never stop doing good to them. (Jeremiah 32:40)
- I will tell of the kindnesses of the LORD, the deeds for which he is to be praised, according to all the LORD has done for us—yes, the

many good things he has done for Israel, according to his compassion and many kindnesses. (Isaiah 63:7)

## CHAPTER 3: THE BEST YEAR EVER

- The Spirit of the Lord is on me, because he has anointed me to proclaim good news to the poor. He has sent me to proclaim freedom for the prisoners and recovery of sight for the blind, to set the oppressed free, to proclaim the year of the Lord's favor. (Luke 4:18–19)
- For God so loved the world that he gave his one and only Son, that whoever believes in him shall not perish but have eternal life. (John 3:16)
- For he says, "In the time of my favor I heard you, and in the day of salvation I helped you." I tell you, now is the time of God's favor, now is the day of salvation. (2 Corinthians 6:2)
- For his anger lasts only a moment, but his favor lasts a lifetime; weeping may stay for the night, but rejoicing comes in the morning. (Psalm 30:5)

## CHAPTER 4: NO, REALLY, IT'S TRUE

- Go, eat your food with gladness, and drink your wine with a joyful heart, for it is now that God favors what you do. (Ecclesiastes 9:7, NIV 1984)
- For God's gifts and his call are irrevocable. (Romans 11:29)

## CHAPTER 5: ESTABLISHED IN GRACE

- All of us also lived among them at one time, gratifying the cravings of our flesh and following its desires and thoughts. Like the rest, we were by nature deserving of wrath. But because of his great love for us, God, who is rich in mercy, made us alive with Christ even when we were dead in transgressions—it is by grace you have been saved. (Ephesians 2:3–5)

- And my God will supply all your needs according to His riches in glory in Christ Jesus. (Philippians 4:19, NASB)

## CHAPTER 6: WHAT ABOUT MONDAYS?

- You have allowed me to suffer much hardship, but you will restore me to life again and lift me up from the depths of the earth. You will restore me to even greater honor and comfort me once again. (Psalm 71:20–21, NLT)

## CHAPTER 7: HEAVEN'S NEPOTISM

- "I will be a Father to you, and you will be my sons and daughters," says the Lord Almighty. (2 Corinthians 6:18)
- Be strong and courageous. Do not be afraid or terrified because of them, for the LORD your God goes with you; he will never leave you nor forsake you. (Deuteronomy 31:6)
- Keep your lives free from the love of money and be content with what you have, because God has said, "Never will I leave you; never will I forsake you." (Hebrews 13:5)
- If you then, who are evil, know how to give good gifts to your children, how much more will your Father who is in heaven give good things to those who ask him! (Matthew 7:11, ESV)
- And now that you belong to Christ, you are the true children of Abraham. You are his heirs, and God's promise to Abraham belongs to you. (Galatians 3:29, NLT)

## CHAPTER 8: ABRAHAM'S HEIRS

- In your seed all the nations of the earth shall be blessed, because you have obeyed My voice. (Genesis 22:18)

- Blessed (happy, fortunate, prosperous, and enviable) is the man who walks *and* lives not in the counsel of the ungodly [following their advice, their plans and purposes]. (Psalm 1:1, AMP)
- And Jabez called on the God of Israel saying, "Oh, that You would bless me indeed, and enlarge my territory, that Your hand would be with me, and that You would keep me from evil, that I may not cause pain!" So God granted him what he requested. (1 Chronicles 4:10, NKJV)
- A feast is made for laughter, wine makes life merry, and money is the answer for everything. (Ecclesiastes 10:19)
- And the second is like it: "Love your neighbor as yourself." (Matthew 22:39)
- All these blessings will come on you and accompany you if you obey the LORD your God: You will be blessed in the city and blessed in the country. The fruit of your womb will be blessed, and the crops of your land and the young of your livestock—the calves of your herds and the lambs of your flocks. Your basket and your kneading trough will be blessed. You will be blessed when you come in and blessed when you go out. (Deuteronomy 28:2–6)
- Whatever you do, work at it with all your heart, as working for the Lord. (Colossians 3:23)
- I will bless you; I will make your name great, and you will be a blessing. . . . All peoples on earth will be blessed through you. (Genesis 12:2–3, NIV 1984)

## CHAPTER 9: GOOD EYES

- Now faith is confidence in what we hope for and assurance about what we do not see. (Hebrews 11:1)
- The lamp of the body is the eye. Therefore, when your eye is good, your whole body also is full of light. But when

*your eye* is bad, your body also *is* full of darkness. (Luke 11:34, NKJV)

- I pray that the eyes of your heart may be enlightened in order that you may know the hope to which he has called you, the riches of his glorious inheritance in his holy people. (Ephesians 1:18)

## CHAPTER 10: WHAT YOU GET IS WHAT YOU SEE

- Surely, LORD, you bless the righteous; you surround them with your favor as with a shield. (Psalm 5:12)
- You intended to harm me, but God intended it for good to accomplish what is now being done, the saving of many lives. (Genesis 50:20)
- The eye is the lamp of the body. If your eyes are healthy, your whole body will be full of light. (Matthew 6:22)
- The lamp of the body is the eye. Therefore, when your eye is good, your whole body also is full of light. But when *your eye* is bad, your body also *is* full of darkness. (Luke 11:34, NKJV)

## CHAPTER 11: A FAVOR-FRIENDLY MIND

- For as he thinks within himself, so he is. (Proverbs 23:7, NASB)
- Wherefore gird up the loins of your mind, be sober, and hope to the end for the grace that is to be brought unto you. (1 Peter 1:13, KJV)
- Do not conform to the pattern of this world, but be transformed by the renewing of your mind. Then you will be able to test and approve what God's will is—his good, pleasing and perfect will. (Romans 12:2)
- She said to herself, "If only I touch his cloak, I will be healed." (Matthew 9:21)

- Finally, brothers and sisters, whatever is true, whatever is noble, whatever is right, whatever is pure, whatever is lovely, whatever is admirable—if anything is excellent or praiseworthy—think about such things. (Philippians 4:8)

## CHAPTER 12: WHAT ABOUT "IF"?

- I have told you these things, so that in me you may have peace. In this world you will have trouble. But take heart! I have overcome the world. (John 16:33)
- We have this hope as an anchor for the soul, firm and secure. It enters the inner sanctuary behind the curtain. (Hebrews 6:19)
- Hope deferred makes the heart sick, but a longing fulfilled is a tree of life. (Proverbs 13:12)
- I remain confident of this: I will see the goodness of the LORD in the land of the living. (Psalm 27:13)

## CHAPTER 13: CHAPTERS

- And we know that in all things God works for the good of those who love him, who have been called according to his purpose. (Romans 8:28)
- Moses said to them, "It is the bread the LORD has given you to eat. This is what the LORD has commanded: 'Everyone is to gather as much as they need. . . .'" The Israelites did as they were told; some gathered much, some little. . . . Then Moses said to them, "No one is to keep any of it until morning." However, some of them paid no attention to Moses; they kept part of it until morning, but it was full of maggots and began to smell. (Exodus 16:15–17, 19–20)
- The rabble with them began to crave other food, and again the Israelites started wailing and said, "If only we had meat to eat! We

remember the fish we ate in Egypt at no cost—also the cucumbers, melons, leeks, onions and garlic. But now we have lost our appetite; we never see anything but this manna!" (Numbers 11:4–6)

- This is the day the Lord has made; we will rejoice and be glad in it. (Psalm 118:24, NKJV)
- As yet I am as strong this day as I was in the day that Moses sent me: as my strength was then, even so is my strength now, for war, both to go out, and to come in. Now therefore give me this mountain, whereof the LORD spake in that day; for thou heardest in that day how the Anakims were there, and that the cities were great and fenced: if so be the LORD will be with me, then I shall be able to drive them out, as the LORD said. (Joshua 14:11–12, KJV)
- I will make you into a great nation, and I will bless you; I will make your name great, and you will be a blessing. (Genesis 12:2)
- The LORD will watch over your coming and going both now and forevermore. (Psalm 121:8)

## CHAPTER 14: FAVOR FORWARD

- David asked, "Is there anyone still left of the house of Saul to whom I can show kindness for Jonathan's sake?"(2 Samuel 9:1)
- So King David had him brought from Lo Debar, from the house of Makir son of Ammiel. When Mephibosheth son of Jonathan, the son of Saul, came to David, he bowed down to pay him honor. David said, "Mephibosheth!" "At your service," he replied. "Don't be afraid," David said to him, "for I will surely show you kindness for the sake of your father Jonathan. I will restore to you all the land that belonged to your grandfather Saul, and you will always eat at my table." (2 Samuel 9:5–7)

## CHAPTER 15: FAVOR DYNAMICS

- Jesus grew in wisdom and stature, and in favor with God and man. (Luke 2:52)

- "O Lord, please hear my prayer! Heed the prayers of those of us who delight to honor you. Please help me now as I go in and ask the king for a great favor—put it into his heart to be kind to me." (I was the king's cupbearer.) (Nehemiah 1:11, TLB)

- From the east I summon a bird of prey; from a far-off land, a man to fulfill my purpose. What I have said, that I will bring about; what I have planned, that I will do. (Isaiah 46:11)

- The one who guards a fig tree will eat its fruit, and whoever protects their master will be honored. (Proverbs 27:18)

- As iron sharpens iron, so one person sharpens another. (Proverbs 27:17)

- Good people obtain favor from the LORD, but he condemns those who devise wicked schemes. (Proverbs 12:2)

- Then you will win favor and a good name in the sight of God and man. (Proverbs 3:4)

## CHAPTER 16: FAVOR SHIFTS

- Simon answered, "Master, we've worked hard all night and haven't caught anything. But because you say so, I will let down the nets." When they had done so, they caught such a large number of fish that their nets began to break. So they signaled their partners in the other boat to come and help them, and they came and filled both boats so full that they began to sink. (Luke 5:5–7)

- Now when he had left speaking, he said unto Simon, Launch out into the deep, and let down your nets for a draught. (Luke 5:4, KJV)

- The angel of God that had been leading the camp of Israel now shifted and got behind them. And the Pillar of Cloud that had been in front also shifted to the rear. The Cloud was now between the camp of Egypt and the camp of Israel. The Cloud enshrouded one camp in darkness and flooded the other with light. The two camps didn't come near each other all night. (Exodus 14:19–20, MSG)
- I have told you these things, so that in me you may have peace. In this world you will have trouble. But take heart! I have overcome the world. (John 16:33)
- The tongue has the power of life and death, and those who love it will eat its fruit. (Proverbs 18:21)
- "For I know the plans I have for you," declares the LORD, "plans to prosper you and not to harm you, plans to give you hope and a future." (Jeremiah 29:11)
- Then said the LORD unto me, "Thou hast well seen: for I will hasten my word to perform it." (Jeremiah 1:12, KJV)

## CHAPTER 17: FAVOR FORECASTS

- For the LORD God is a sun and shield; the LORD bestows favor and honor; no good thing does he withhold from those whose walk is blameless. (Psalm 84:11)
- "For I know the plans I have for you," declares the LORD, "plans to prosper you and not to harm you, plans to give you hope and a future." (Jeremiah 29:11)
- Do not fret because of those who are evil or be envious of those who do wrong; for like the grass they will soon wither, like green plants they will soon die away. Trust in the LORD and do good; dwell in the land and enjoy safe pasture. Take delight in the LORD, and he will give you the desires of your heart. (Psalm 37:1–4)

- This day I call the heavens and the earth as witnesses against you that I have set before you life and death, blessings and curses. Now choose life, so that you and your children may live. (Deuteronomy 30:19)
- Gracious words are a honeycomb, sweet to the soul and healing to the bones. (Proverbs 16:24)
- Through the blessing of the upright a city is exalted, but by the mouth of the wicked it is destroyed. (Proverbs 11:11)
- From the fruit of their lips people enjoy good things, but the unfaithful have an appetite for violence. (Proverbs 13:2)
- Beat your plowshares into swords and your pruninghooks into spears: let the weak say, I am strong! (Joel 3:10 , KJV)
- I can do all things through Christ who strengthens me. (Philippians 4:13, NKJV).
- "The LORD who rescued me from the paw of the lion and the paw of the bear will rescue me from the hand of this Philistine." Saul said to David, "Go, and the LORD be with you." (1 Samuel 17:37)
- David said to the Philistine, "You come against me with sword and spear and javelin, but I come against you in the name of the LORD Almighty, the God of the armies of Israel, whom you have defied. This day the LORD will deliver you into my hands, and I'll strike you down and cut off your head. This very day I will give the carcasses of the Philistine army to the birds and the wild animals, and the whole world will know that there is a God in Israel. All those gathered here will know that it is not by sword or spear that the LORD saves; for the battle is the LORD's, and he will give all of you into our hands." (1 Samuel 17:45–47)
- "No weapon forged against you will prevail, and you will refute every tongue that accuses you. This is the heritage of the servants of the LORD, and this is their vindication from me," declares the LORD. (Isaiah 54:17)

## CHAPTER 18: DON'T SETTLE IN SPAIN

- Planted in the house of the LORD, they will flourish in the courts of our God. (Psalm 92:13)
- Terah took his son Abram, his grandson Lot son of Haran, and his daughter-in-law Sarai, the wife of his son Abram, and together they set out from Ur of the Chaldeans to go to Canaan. But when they came to Haran, they settled there. (Genesis 11:31)
- We must pay the most careful attention, therefore, to what we have heard, so that we do not drift away. (Hebrews 2:1)
- We have this hope as an anchor for the soul, firm and secure. It enters the inner sanctuary behind the curtain where our forerunner, Jesus, has entered on our behalf. (Hebrews 6:19)

## CHAPTER 19: THE UNFINISHED WORKS OF GOD

- Being confident of this, that he who began a good work in you will carry it on to completion until the day of Christ Jesus. (Philippians 1:6)
- For we are God's handiwork, created in Christ Jesus to do good works, which God prepared in advance for us to do. (Ephesians 2:10)
- They devoted themselves to the apostles' teaching and to fellowship, to the breaking of bread and to prayer. (Acts 2:42)
- Rejoice always, pray continually, give thanks in all circumstances; for this is God's will for you in Christ Jesus. (1 Thessalonians 5:16–18)

## CLOSING

- If you then, who are evil, know how to give good gifts to your children, how much more will your Father who is in heaven give good things to those who ask him! (Matthew 7:11, ESV)

# Appendix 2: Takeaway Quotes from Each Chapter

## CHAPTER 1: AM I SEEING CLEARLY?

- There's a huge difference in assuming God is good and seeing evidence of his goodness.
- God is the source of all goodness and good things.
- The more good we see, the more optimistic we will be.

## CHAPTER 2: NO MORE TURNING

- Wrong assumptions are the termites of trust in our relationship with God.
- The actual challenge for us is not *gaining* God's approval but rather *accepting* God's approval.
- Stop *seeking* God's approval and start *accepting* God's favor.

## CHAPTER 3: THE BEST YEAR EVER

- The cross is a symbol of God's never-ending, ongoing favor to all mankind.
- You don't have to worry about falling out of favor because of a failure!
- We are conditioned by life to seek approval, which means we live from the premise that we don't have it.
- God's favor is forever.

## CHAPTER 4: NO, REALLY, IT'S TRUE

- Rather than performing for God's approval, live as if you already have it!

- Even when God doesn't approve of what you've done, he still approves of you!
- Nothing about the way he sees you changes. Nothing!

## CHAPTER 5: ESTABLISHED IN GRACE

- Favor is the outworking of God's grace.
- God's mercy doesn't give us what we deserve, and God's favor gives us what we don't deserve.
- Grace is the unmerited favor of God.
- Favor can't be fair because life isn't fair.

## CHAPTER 6: WHAT ABOUT MONDAYS?

- Metaphorically there are only two days a week: there's Sunday when God's favor is obvious, and there's Monday when God's favor feels absent.
- The path of favor is not always on the mountaintop; it also winds through the valley.
- Sunday's favor doesn't stop with Monday's challenges.
- God's undeserved goodness is not just equal to the undeserved hardship; it is surpassing in greatness.

## CHAPTER 7: HEAVEN'S NEPOTISM

- God saw you and blessed you before you showed up on the earth.
- Favor is not based on *who* we are but on *whose* we are.
- Heaven's nepotism is something to be *chosen*. It's an *opportunity given to us,* but it is *conveyed to us based on our choosing it.*

## CHAPTER 8: ABRAHAM'S HEIRS

- God wants us to pray for our financial needs with the same ease that we pray blessing on our food.

- A compartmentalized life may offer more control but less capacity.
- When we put God in the center we can see how it is all intended to be.
- The Hebrew word for "work" and "worship" is the same word—*avodah*.
- God gives humans the opportunity to work as a way of including us in his creative process.

## CHAPTER 9: GOOD EYES

- The only thing that's different between a negative person and a positive person is what they "see."
- You don't have to deny the realities associated with life being hard to see the realities associated with God being good!
- All of us have the potential to see less of what we don't want to see and more of what we become intentional about seeing.
- God's goodness isn't hidden, and neither is God's favor making limited appearances in our lives.

## CHAPTER 10: WHAT YOU GET IS WHAT YOU SEE

- Focus more on what's right about God rather than what's wrong with the world.
- When you start looking for good things, you realize they are sometimes found in unlikely places.
- Favor surrounds us. It's in front, behind, above, and on both sides of us.
- No matter what your perspective on life, you're not stuck with it.
- Good is synonymous with God.

## CHAPTER 11: A FAVOR-FRIENDLY MIND

- Nothing increases favor in our lives like thinking favor and expecting favor.

- No matter what our age, we have the ability to *change the habits of our mind.*
- Think favor so you can open up the search engine in your mind for favor.
- When you are favor minded, you will find more favor.
- What we attract into our lives is not based on what we want but on what's inside of us.
- What's in you is more important than what's around you.
- Always think something good to yourself.
- Keep your mind on the favor not the failure, the joy not the pain, and the prize not the price.

## CHAPTER 12: WHAT ABOUT "IF"?

- The greatest struggles in life are not the hardships themselves but the questions that the hardships create.
- Life is hard; God is good.
- Hope is the "expectation of good."
- Hope begins when we stop *wondering* and start *watching.*
- Hope is a stubborn, unrelenting determination to not allow the hardships of life to downsize the bigness of God.
- Stop trying to answer the "why" and start eliminating the "if."

## CHAPTER 13: CHAPTERS

- If I could have a do-over, I would *fight* to keep that painful, difficult, frustrating event as a chapter in my life.
- Some of the worst chapters make the best stories.
- God never writes us off because of bad chapters.
- What some see as a reason to be bitter, others see as an opportunity to be better.

- Yesterday's favor is not today's favor.
- God's favor was on yesterday, yesterday—it's not on yesterday, today!

## CHAPTER 14: FAVOR FORWARD

- The greatest expression of gratitude we have is to pay it forward.
- Our story is a story of God's extravagant favor.
- God decided that nothing about us disqualifies us.

## CHAPTER 15: FAVOR DYNAMICS

- Right now God has people in your life that are the expression of his favor toward you.
- Often God's favor comes through the people we least expect it from.
- Be confident and secure in knowing that God has favor reserved with your name on it.
- God will use the greatness in other people to bring out the greatness in us.
- Nothing and no one can stop God's favor in your life!

## CHAPTER 16: FAVOR SHIFTS

- When God asks us to do something out of the ordinary, it is because he wants to do something out of the ordinary for us.
- Sometimes God wants you to keep doing what you're doing, but he wants you to do it in a different way.
- Sometimes the shift we need to make is to get our minds off the past and on to the future.
- Favor is God giving us an advantage in life when facing a disadvantage.
- Just because you can't see something happening doesn't mean that nothing is happening.

## CHAPTER 17: FAVOR FORECASTS

- Forecasting favor is using your voice to predict favor in your future.
- Forecast favor according to your *faith,* not your *feelings* or *fears.*
- You can be authentic about challenges and weaknesses and still proclaim your confidence.
- Words are carriers of God's plan and activate God's will.

## CHAPTER 18: DON'T SETTLE IN SPAIN

- It's a common tendency for people to settle in their own version of Spain.
- When priorities like faith, family, and fitness are settled they serve as a strong foundation for a life of favor.
- Settled passion will hinder God's favor.
- Sometimes people are supposed to stay *where* they have been, but nothing is supposed to stay *like* it has been.
- Drifting is not a direction.
- The unanchored soul will drift.

## CHAPTER 19: THE UNFINISHED WORKS OF GOD

- God's not dead and God's not done!
- Sometimes God has to make us bigger on the inside before he can bring increase on the outside.
- Limits are broken and lids are lifted by people who have big dreams.
- If we want to experience all that God has for us, we need to keep our minds open to the possibilities that seem impossible.
- *His favor lasts a lifetime!*

## CLOSING

- We have an incredibly generous Father who has unending favor.
- We have every reason to remain confident in the goodness of God.

# Notes

1. Brennan Manning, *The Ragamuffin Gospel* (Colorado Springs: Multnomah, 2005), 24.
2. Robert Thiele and George David Weiss. Copyright Abilene Music Inc., Range Road Music Inc., Quartet Music.
3. *Strong's Concordance,* Greek word 1680, "elpis" is defined in part as the "expectation of good," www.blueletterbible.org/lang/lexicon /lexicon.cfm?Strongs=G1680&t=KJV.
4. See Psalm 71:20–21.
5. *Huffington Post,* Healthy Living section, November 19, 2014.
6. Lyrics and music by Barry Mann, Cynthia Weil, and Phil Spector. Performed by The Righteous Brothers. Copyright ABKCO Music Inc.